AROUND THE YEAR

Knowledge and understanding of the world
Seasonal activities

Sally Gray

Seasonal ideas ◆ Festival activities ◆ Early learning goals

CREDITS

British Library Cataloguing-in-Publication Data
A catalogue record for this book is available from the British Library.

ISBN 0 439 01908 7

AUTHOR
Sally Gray

EDITOR
Lesley Sudlow

ASSISTANT EDITOR
Saverla Mezzana

SERIES DESIGNER
Anna Oliwa

DESIGNER
Anna Oliwa

ILLUSTRATIONS
Anna Hopkins

COVER ILLUSTRATION
Anna Hopkins

ACKNOWLEDGEMENTS
The publishers gratefully acknowledge permission to reproduce the following copyright material:

Trevor Harvey for 'Autumn is here' by Trevor Harvey © 2001 Trevor Harvey, previously unpublished; **Barbara Moore** for 'The ugly duckling', a retelling of a Hans Christian Andersen story, 'The story of Holi', a retelling of a traditional story, 'The story of Baisakhi', a retelling of a traditional story, 'The story of Divali', a retelling of a traditional story, and 'Chinese New Year', a retelling of a traditional story, by Barbara Moore © 2001 Barbara Moore, all previously unpublished.

Text © 2001 Sally Gray
© 2001 Scholastic Ltd

Published by Scholastic Ltd, Villiers House, Clarendon Avenue, Leamington Spa, Warwickshire CV32 5PR

Designed using Adobe Pagemaker
Printed by Proost NV, Belgium

Visit our website at www.scholastic.co.uk

1 2 3 4 5 6 7 8 9 0   1 2 3 4 5 6 7 8 9 0

INTRODUCTION
5 Around the year

BACKGROUND INFORMATION
7 Festivals

SPRING
9 Mad March hares
10 Yellow flowers
11 Spring-cleaning
12 The ugly duckling
13 Signs of spring
14 Nest-building
15 Leaf prints (St Patrick's Day)
16 All things wonderful (Mother's Day)
17 Wiggling snakes (Holi)
18 A nest egg (Easter)
19 Parting the sea (Pesach/Passover)
20 Leader of the day (Baisakhi)
21 Flower festival (Hanamatsuri)
22 Days gone by (May Day)

SUMMER
23 Summer mobiles
24 Holiday time
25 Summer fête
26 Keeping cool
27 Beach huts
28 A perfect place
29 Lights and lanterns (Wesak)
30 Making a mark (Shavuot)
31 Processions and parades
(Midsummer's Day)
32 Special memories (Father's Day)
33 Shape biscuits (Father's Day)
34 The best boat
(Dragon Boat Festival)
35 Keeping dry (St Swithun's Day)
36 Caring for others
(Raksha Bandhan)

CONTENTS

AUTUMN
37 Helping squirrel
38 Autumn colours
39 Leaf models
40 Collect the leaves
41 Preparing for winter
42 Hibernating habits
43 Drums (Ethiopian New Year)
44 Memory lane (Grandparent's Day)
45 Shelters (Sukkot)
46 Farm machines (Harvest Festival)
47 The thick jungle (Divali)
48 Going fishing (St Andrew's Day)
49 Free kitchen
   (Guru Nanak's birthday)
50 Model temple (Hanukkah)

WINTER
51 Winter soup
52 All about ice
53 Winter birds
54 Light and heat
55 Pop-up snowman
56 Winter clothes game
57 Sunrise and sunset (Ramadan)
58 Computer calendars (Advent)
59 Looking after Santa
   (Christmas Day)
60 All about Eid (Eid-ul-Fitr)
61 Millennium Eve (New Year)
62 Sand maps (Chinese New Year)
63 All about weddings
   (Valentine's Day)
64 Animal parade
   (Mardi Gras/Shrove Tuesday)

PHOTOCOPIABLES
65 The ugly duckling
66 The story of Holi (Holi)
67 The story of Baisakhi (Baisakhi)
68 Days gone by (May Day)
69 Keeping cool
70 Lights and lanterns (Wesak)
71 Keeping dry (St Swithun's Day)
72 Autumn is here
73 Leaf models
74 Shelters (Sukkot)
75 The story of Divali (Divali)
76 Free kitchen
   (Guru Nanak's birthday)
77 Winter birds
78 Pop-up snowman
79 Winter clothes game
80 Chinese New Year
   (Chinese New Year)

Around the year

The aims of this series

This book forms part of a series of six books that provide practical activities to support the Early Learning Goals (QCA). Each book focuses on a different area of learning. The ideas presented can be applied equally well to the documents on pre-school education published for Scotland, Wales and Northern Ireland.

As the title of the series suggests, the books are intended to be used throughout the year, with activities and ideas for each of the four seasons and the multicultural festivals and special days that fall within them.

The teaching of the seasons and their associated activities has long been established as an important part of early learning. The ideas contained in these books provide new and interesting twists to the familiar themes of the seasons, and they also consider some of the most popular and less well-known multicultural festivals and feast days. Practitioners will find the activities an invaluable source of new ideas that can be dipped into at any time throughout the year.

Knowledge and understanding of the world

In this book you will find activities that cover in detail all the aspects of the area of learning for Knowledge and understanding of the world. The children will be encouraged to find out about past events in their own lives and those of their families (see 'Special memories' on page 32); they will use information technology to support their learning (see 'Computer calendars' on page 58) and they will find out about and identify some features of living things and the natural world (see 'Mad March hares' on page 9).

How to use this book

The book is divided into four main chapters – one for each of the seasons. For the purpose of the book, the seasons are divided as follows:

◆ Spring (March, April and May)
◆ Summer (June, July and August)
◆ Autumn (September, October and November)
◆ Winter (December, January and February).

Each chapter provides 14 activities (one per page). Six of these activities are linked specifically to the particular season, and the other eight activities are linked to the festivals associated with that time of year. The teaching of the festivals has been approached in a number of different ways. At times, the underlying themes of the festivals, such as leadership, caring for others and families, have been highlighted in the activity suggestions. Other activities provide opportunities to learn about a range of cultures and traditions.

Each activity page provides a comprehensive list of the resources needed, any preparation required and a step-by-step guide of how to teach and manage the work. Where an activity involves cooking or handling of food, this symbol ⟨!⟩ will remind you to check for any allergies and dietary requirements.

There is also a useful two-page section providing a summary of information about the festivals covered in this book. This, alongside the information contained in the activity chapters and photocopiable stories, provides a basic background to the festivals, although it is not intended to be exhaustive.

Supporting and extending the learning

Although the activities are aimed at four-year-olds, the 'Support' section gives suggestions about how the main activity can be adapted for younger children or those with special needs, and the 'Extension' section explains how the main activity can be extended for older or more able children. The extension ideas may also include suggestions for follow-up activities to continue, extend or reinforce the children's learning.

Using the photocopiable sheets

There are 16 photocopiable sheets that provide a range of resources to back-up the activities. They cover a variety of different learning opportunities. Some are stories or poems linked to specific festivals or seasonal activities, such as 'Holi' on page 66 and 'Autumn is here' on page 72, while others are intended to be used to promote discussion, such as 'Shelters (Sukkot)' on page 74. Several of the photocopiable sheets are to be used as templates and games, such as 'Winter clothes game' on page 79, and others can be used as the basis for a group discussion, such as 'Days gone by (May Day)' on page 68.

In addition, some of the photocopiable sheets are suitable for enlarging, sending home to reinforce the children's learning with their parents or carers, or using as a record of the children's work.

Links with home

For each activity there are suggestions for 'home links' – ways of linking the work to the children's home environment, including how to involve parents and carers in the children's learning. This partnership with parents and carers is an important way to provide continuity with the children's home lives.

The children will benefit enormously from having their learning reinforced at home, and it is valuable for parents and carers to understand the learning potential of their children's play and everyday activities.

In addition, it would be very useful to enlist the help of parents and carers for many of the activities performed regularly in your group setting.

Festivals

St Patrick's Day (17 March)
An Irish celebration of their patron saint who rid Ireland of all snakes. Shamrock is worn (St Patrick used it to explain the Christian belief in the Holy Trinity).

Mother's Day (March/April)
Once a holiday for servant girls to visit their mothers with gifts, it is now a time to show love and appreciation to mothers.

Holi (March/April)
This Hindu festival remembers Prahlada who refused to worship the king regardless of the punishment. Holi traditions today include throwing paint and coloured water over each other.

Easter (March/April)
The most important Christian festival when Jesus' return to life is celebrated. People give chocolate eggs as a symbol of new life.

Pesach/Passover (March/April)
An eight-day Jewish festival commemorating the Jews' exodus from slavery in Egypt. A traditional meal called Seder is eaten.

Baisakhi (14 April)
The Sikh New Year festival commemorating the five volunteers that offered to sacrifice themselves at Guru Gobind Singh's request. Also marks the introduction of the Khalsa.

Hanamatsuri (April)
A Japanese flower festival celebrating the birth of Buddha. Baby Buddha images are placed in floral shrines symbolizing the garden in which the Buddha was born.

May Day (1 May)
In Roman and Celtic times, May Day celebrated the goddess Flora. Traditions include dancing around a maypole, processions and selecting a May queen.

Wesak (May/June)
Theravada Buddhists celebrate the birth, enlightenment and death of the Buddha on this day. People decorate their temples and homes with candles, flowers and incense.

Shavuot (May/June)
A Jewish festival celebrating the revelation of the Ten Commandments to Moses on Mount Sinai. Synagogues are decorated with flowers and dairy foods.

Midsummer's Day (24 June)
Falls shortly after the longest day of the year. Druids still meet at Stonehenge for sunrise. Traditions include bonfires, feasts and torchlit processions.

Father's Day (June)
Children give love and thanks to their fathers during this modern festival.

Dragon Boat Festival (June)
A Chinese festival honouring Ch'u Yuan who drowned himself in protest at the Emperor. Today dragon boat races symbolize the rush to save him.

St Swithun's Day (15 July)
Legend says that if it rains on this day it will continue to do so for 40 days and nights.

Raksha Bandhan (July/August)
A Hindu festival when girls tie a rakhi (bracelet) around their brothers' wrists to protect them, and the brothers promise to protect their sisters.

Ethiopian New Year (11 September)
Celebrated by Rastafarians. Each year in the four-year cycle is named after an evangelist. Celebrations include eating, drumming and dancing.

Grandparent's Day (September)
This is a modern festival in which children and families thank their grandparents by making cards and sending them gifts.

Sukkot (September/October)
A Jewish festival that commemorates the people's journey in the wilderness after escaping from Egypt. Temporary shelters are built and harvest is celebrated.

Harvest Festival (September/October)
A time of thanksgiving for the harvesting of crops. Traditions include harvest suppers and giving of food to the needy.

Divali (October/November)
Hindus remember the story of Rama and Sita. Sikhs celebrate the sixth Guru, Guru Hargobind's escape from imprisonment. Homes are decorated with divas (lamps).

St Andrew's Day (30 November)
A Scottish celebration of their patron saint. A traditional meal of haggis, neeps and tatties is eaten by many Scottish families.

Guru Nanak's birthday (November)
Sikh festival celebrating the birthday of the founder of the faith. Families meet at the gurdwara to hear readings made from the holy book and to sing hymns about the life of the first Guru. A meal is shared from the free kitchen and distributed to the poor and needy.

Hanukkah (November/December)
Jewish festival of light lasting eight days, commemorating the reclamation of the temple from the Syrians and the miracle of the temple light that burned for eight days on a small amount of oil. For eight evenings, one candle is lit, from right to left in a hanukiah (nine-branched menorah). Children play a game of dreidel.

Ramadan (November/December)
A Muslim period of fasting that lasts for one month. During this month, adults do not eat between sunrise and sunset and think of others who are less fortunate than themselves.

Advent (December)
Christian period of preparation for Jesus' birth, beginning on the fourth Sunday before Christmas and ending on Christmas Day. Traditions include Advent candles and calendars.

Christmas Day (25 December)
Christian festival celebrating the birth of Jesus. People decorate their homes and exchange gifts as a reminder of those given to Jesus.

Eid-ul-Fitr (December/January)
Muslim festival held at the end of Ramadan. People wear new clothes, visit family and friends, exchange gifts and cards and eat a celebratory meal.

New Year (1 January)
New Year is celebrated with parties and the traditional singing of 'Auld Lang Syne'. People reflect on the past and make resolutions for the future.

Chinese New Year (January/February)
The most important Chinese festival, lasting 15 days. Families clean and decorate their homes, wear new clothes and visit their friends and family.

Valentine's Day (14 February)
The patron saint of lovers' day is celebrated by sending anonymous cards and gifts to loved ones. Valentine was probably a roman soldier that refused to agree not to marry.

Mardi Gras/Shrove Tuesday (February/March)
Falls on the day before the Christian period of Lent. People use up certain foods to make pancakes. Celebrations include an elaborate carnival.

Mad March hares

What you need
Information books showing pictures of hares and other British wildlife; strips of white paper and brown tissue paper; pink card; a template of hare-shaped ears; scissors; papier-mâché paste in a bucket; glue and spreaders; ribbons or elastic; a balloon per pair of children; stapler.

Preparation
Blow up a balloon for each pair of children.

What to do
Share some information books about British wildlife, in particular mammals, and show the children some pictures of hares. Explain that hares live in the open countryside, unlike rabbits that nest in burrows under the ground. During springtime, and especially in March and April, they can be seen in fields and the countryside. Mother hares have several litters each year and many baby hares (leverets) are born in the spring. People talk about 'mad March hares' because at this time the adults can frequently be seen 'boxing' and the young hares are often very lively – they may 'streak' or run very fast, leap in the air, jump over each other and twist and turn in mid-air.

Explain to the children that they are going to make their own hare hats. Provide pairs of children with an inflated balloon and strips of white paper and paste. Ask them to cover the balloon with three or four layers of pasted strips of paper. Make a final layer of brown tissue paper strips. Let the balloons dry overnight.

Meanwhile, help each child to cut out two 'hare' ears from pink card, using a template. Cover one side of the ears with more strips of brown tissue paper, pasted on lightly.

Once the balloons are dry, cut them in half to make two caps, removing the rubber fragments. Help the children to staple the ears to the sides of their caps and add ribbons or elastic for tying the caps under their chins.

Support
Help the children to use the correct amount of paste, and attach the ears and ribbons for them.

Extension
Encourage the children to use the caps for some dance work, pretending to be baby March hares, twisting and turning, jumping and running.

Learning objectives
To find out about and identify some features of living things; to build and construct with papier mâché.

Group size
Pairs of children in small groups.

Home links
Let the children wear their caps at home-time and encourage them to tell (or show) their parents and carers what they have learned about hares.

Yellow flowers

Learning objective
To find out about and identify features in the natural world.

Group size
Whole group for walk; small groups for activity.

What you need
Pictures and examples of yellow spring flowers (from your own garden or bought from a shop); sketchbooks; pencils; yellow, green, red and white paints; mixing palettes; aprons; paintbrushes; paper; extra helpers.

Preparation
Arrange for some extra helpers to accompany you on a springtime walk to a local park or gardens. Choose a time when there is an abundance of yellow flowers such as daffodils, celandine, primroses and cowslips.

What to do
Discuss the signs of spring with the children. Have they noticed any changes? Talk about how the evenings are getting lighter, how there are more birds singing and how plants and flowers are growing. Show the children the examples of yellow flowers that you have collected and talk about the different shapes of the leaves and petals. Remind them that they must never pick wild flowers as this is against the law.

Home links
Ask parents and carers to help their children to look out for other spring flowers as they come into bloom, such as cow parsley, bluebells, tulips and red campion.

If possible, take the children on a walk to the local park to see the spring flowers. Look out in particular for the yellow flowers that you have already shown them. Can the children remember their names? Once again, look carefully at the different shapes of the leaves and petals. Give each child a sketchbook and pencil and encourage them to draw a selection of the flowers.

Back at your setting, set up a display of some of the yellow flowers. Give each child an apron and provide them with a range of coloured paints and mixing palettes. Encourage them to try to mix the exact tones of yellow that they can see, for example, by adding white or a touch of red. Give each child a sheet of paper and ask them to carefully paint a picture of their chosen flower, reminding them of the shapes of the leaves and petals.

Support
Work closely with the children, showing them how to mix the paints to create a range of yellows. Describe the colours as you make them, using words such as 'pale', 'dark' and so on.

Extension
Ask the children to label their paintings with the flower's name and the words 'petals', 'leaves' and 'stalks'.

Spring-cleaning

What you need
A selection of cleaning items of a variety of textures, such as dustpan and brush, sponge, mop, bucket, scrubbing brush, duster and so on.

Preparation
Make sure that your room is not too tidy! It is best to carry out this activity towards the end of a session.

What to do
Invite the children to sit in a circle with you and ask them to look around the room and think about the things that need cleaning or tidying. For example, the windows may need cleaning, the books in the book corner may need tidying, the paintbrushes and paint pots may need washing; the aprons may need hanging up and so on. Explain that many people like to have a big clean during spring to tidy away the winter things and get ready for the summer-time.

Now, one by one, pass the cleaning items around the circle. Do the children know what each one is and what it can be used for? Have they ever used one

like it? What did they do with it? Ask them to describe how it feels and what it is made of. Encourage each child to try and say something different about it as it is passed around.

Together, think about how each of the items could be used to help spring-clean the room. Give each child, or pair of children, one of the cleaning items and set them a specific task, such as sweeping under the tables, scrubbing the sink, dusting the display table and so on.

Support
Provide a selection of just three or four cleaning items to describe. Show the children how to use each one before they try them out.

Extension
Investigate the best types of liquid and cloths for cleaning windows. Present the children with a range of water from warm to cold – some soapy, some not – and provide paper, rags and sponges. Encourage them to try all the different combinations and discuss what they like or dislike about each one.

Learning objective
To investigate objects and materials.

Group size
Small groups.

Home links
Make badges or stickers for the children that tell of the good work they have done. Let them wear them at home-time and encourage them to tell their parents or carers all about their spring-cleaning efforts!

The ugly duckling

What you need
The photocopiable sheet on page 65; an information book showing pictures of baby and adult animals; pictures of ducklings and cygnets; card; scissors; glue and spreaders; silver foil; yellow pom-poms or cotton-wool balls; tissue paper; coloured card; paints or colouring materials.

What to do
Show the children the information book and use it to generate a discussion about baby animals. Together, describe the baby animals and encourage the children to use the correct names for them, such as foals, piglets, ducklings, kittens and so on. Talk to the children in simple terms about the life cycles of

Show the children some pictures of cygnets, if possible.

Remind the children of the part in the story where the 'ugly duckling' looks at himself in the lake. Explain that this is called a reflection and is similar to looking in a mirror. Have the children ever seen their reflection in anything? (Perhaps in a spoon, a mirror or a pond?)

Now explain to the children that they are going to make their own model of a duckling on a lake. Provide them with a piece of card as a base and a selection of collage materials such as shiny silver foil, yellow cotton-wool balls or pom-poms, coloured card and colouring materials. Invite them to use the materials to make a lake and a fluffy yellow duckling.

Support
Some children will need more guidance than others when designing and making their collage pictures. Demonstrate how to fix the different materials together, and provide as much help as is necessary.

these animals – how they grow from babies to adults and how these adults have babies of their own.

Share the story of 'The ugly duckling' on the photocopiable sheet with the children. Look again at a picture of a real duckling and explain that cygnets are a greyish colour before they grow into beautiful white swans.

Extension
Encourage the children to be creative and add extra details to their lake collages, such as reeds and plants or other animals made from collage, junk or modelling materials.

Signs of spring

What you need
A cassette recorder; camera; photographs of spring flowers, trees in blossom and other spring activities; large pieces of paper; large piece of card folded to make a book cover; colouring and painting materials; stapler; tapestry needle; thread or ribbon; flower press (or heavy books); paper; pencils.

What to do
Talk to the children about the changes that happen at springtime. What things have the children noticed? Encourage them to use their senses to consider all the different signs of spring. What things can they hear? (Bird-song, children playing outside.) What things can they see and smell? (Blossom on trees, spring flowers.)

Explain that you are all going to make a group book about the signs of spring. Together, make a list of the things that the children would like to include such as:
◆ a recording of spring sounds – birds singing, leaves rustling and children playing; make a pocket for the cassette and attach it to the book

◆ pressings of spring flowers that the children bring in from home
◆ photographs of trees in blossom and spring flowers in bloom
◆ observational drawings or paintings of the trees and flowers
◆ shared writing about the group's springtime activities – spring-cleaning, visits to the local park and any new spring-themed songs and stories that they have heard or learned.

Collate all the children's work into a large book made from card. Either sew or staple the pages together. Invite the children to illustrate the cover and decide on a title together.

Support
Provide a structure for the book such as a page of spring flowers, a page of writing about the group's activities and so on. Work with groups and concentrate on completing one page at a time.

Extension
Encourage the children to make their own individual contributions to the book such as a spring poem or story, or a painting of their choice.

Nest-building

What you need
Information books including pictures of different birds' nests; twigs; dried leaves; shredded tissue paper; lengths of wool; Plasticine.

Preparation
If possible, during wintertime, set up a bird-table and feeding station in the grounds of your group.

What to do
Explain to the children that spring is a busy time for many birds. We can hear them singing more as they establish their territories, attract mates and build nests. If we look carefully, we may

notice birds carrying nesting material in their beaks as they fly around. If your group has any nesting boxes in the grounds, the children may be able to see the birds going in and out of them.

Share some information books that show pictures of birds' nests. Look at the various styles and sizes of the nests. Different birds choose different locations for building their nests – on the ground, in hedges, shrubs, trees and nesting boxes. Emphasize the importance of not going near or disturbing birds' nests and how it is against the law to collect any wild birds' eggs.

If possible, visit a park or wildlife reserve to see birds such as swans and moorhens sitting on their nests. Many RSPB reserves are happy to accommodate groups of school children on springtime visits and run excellent educational programmes. (You can access the junior section of the RSPB at their website: www.rspb.org.uk/youth)

Now provide the children with nesting materials such as a selection of twigs, dried leaves, shredded tissue paper, lengths of wool and some Plasticine. Help them to make a nest base from Plasticine and then use the materials to build up a nest (using extra Plasticine to keep the materials in place). Ask them to consider which bird it is for and to think about the size of the nest and where that bird would normally make their nest.

Support
Suggest that the children make small nests, and help them to fix the nesting materials in place.

Extension
Make a display of the children's nests and include information about the different birds.

Leaf prints

What you need

A piece of shamrock (or a picture of a piece); round sponges; green paint; dishes; paintbrushes; aprons; easel or board; pencils; paper; blank card made into greetings cards for the children to stick their paintings onto); glue and spreaders.

Preparation

Cut some printing sponges to the shape of a shamrock leaf.

What to do

Talk to the children about St Patrick, explaining that he is the patron saint of Ireland. Tell them that the shamrock plant is the national symbol of Ireland and that on St Patrick's Day many Irish people wear a sprig of shamrock. Show the children a piece of shamrock, or alternatively a picture of a piece. Count the leaves on the shamrock together and talk about the plant using terms such as stem and leaves.

Ask the children to put on aprons and provide them with green paint in dishes, round sponges, paintbrushes and paper. Explain that you would like them to make a painting of a piece of shamrock. Help them to print the three leaves using the round sponges and

then encourage them to paint on the stem using a paintbrush.

When the paintings are dry, ask the children if they can remember the names of the different parts of the plant. Scribe the words onto an easel or board and ask the children to copy the words onto their paintings, linking the appropriate words to the different parts of the plant with arrows. Attach the children's paintings onto cards and let them send them as St Patrick's Day cards to a friend or relative.

Support

Ask each child to tell you the name of their plant. Can they tell you which are the leaves and which is the stem? Write the words for them and if appropriate ask them to copy them underneath.

Extension

Invite the children to label their paintings without copying the words from the board. Follow up the activity by looking at a selection of other shaped leaves and encouraging the children to make sponge prints or observational paintings of them.

All things wonderful

Learning objective
To investigate objects
and materials by
using all of their
senses.

Group size
Whole group for
discussion; small
groups for activities.

What you need
Material scraps; glue; scissors; strips of
card; ingredients for a simple recipe
such as peppermint creams or biscuits;
tissue paper; crêpe paper; perfume
stick; yoghurt pots; dried pulses;
coloured paper; paints; colouring
materials; blank card made into
greetings cards; paper.

Preparation
Decide on the activities that you are
going to do with the children and
arrange for extra helpers if necessary.
Plan the activities to be carried out over
the course of a week leading up to
Mother's Day.

What to do
Discuss the festival of Mother's Day
sensitively with the children. If any of
the children in your group do not have
regular contact with their mother,
explain that Mother's Day can also be
about paying special attention to
another female who spends time with
them, such as an aunt, a carer,
grandmother and so on.

Explain that you would like the
children to think of things their mothers
or female carers enjoy that appeal to

each of the five senses. For example, ask
the children: 'What things does Mummy
like to taste?' (Chocolate, biscuits, cake
and so on.) 'What things does she like
to smell?' (Perfume, flowers and so on.)
Make a list of the children's ideas.

The week before Mother's Day, set
up five activities linked to each of the

senses, and ensure that the children
make at least one of the objects to give
to their mothers on Mother's Day. Ideas
may include:
◆ Touch – a feely bookmark made
from a variety of material scraps.
◆ Taste – some peppermint creams or
simple biscuits.
◆ Smell – some tissue-paper flowers
rubbed with a perfume stick.
◆ Hearing – a music shaker made from
a yoghurt pot decorated by the children
containing dried lentils or peas.
◆ Sight – a card or picture specially
painted for Mother's Day.

Support
Encourage the children to focus on just
one or two of the senses and the
related activities.

Extension
Invite the children to think of their own
idea of something to make for their
mothers. Ask them to tell you which
sense it is aimed at – is it something to
taste, touch, see, hear or feel?

Home links
Encourage parents
and carers to spend
time discussing the
five senses with their
children. Suggest that
they look around their
home to find
examples of things
that appeal to each of
the five senses.

Wiggling snakes

What you need
The photocopiable sheet on page 66; one adult helper per group (if possible); construction materials; pasta tubes; tapestry needles; thread or ribbon; card; split-pin fasteners; paper; pencils; scissors.

What to do
Read to the children 'The story of Holi' on the photocopiable sheet, emphasizing how Prahlada was spared by the wiggling snakes. Explain that the children are going to make their own wiggling snakes to use when retelling the story. Before the children begin to make their snakes, encourage them to make wiggling movements themselves. Demonstrate how they use their joints such as wrists, fingers, knees and elbows to move in a wiggly fashion. Set out the different materials on separate tables and allocate a helper to

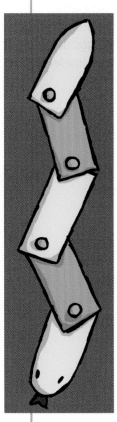

each table if possible. Alternatively, set up the tables at different times of the day or for different sessions and spread the activity out across a few days. The snakes can be made as follows:
◆ Provide a selection of construction materials, such as Meccano, Mobilo and Multilink cubes and challenge the children to make long wiggling snakes.
◆ Supply a box of pasta tubes, tapestry needles and thick thread or ribbons. Help the children to thread the tubes to make long snakes.
◆ Give strips of card and split-pin fasteners and show the children how to fix the strips loosely together to make wiggling snakes.

◆ Distribute paper, pencils and scissors and show the children how to draw and then cut out a spiral shape that wiggles as you hold it up.

Make sure that each type of snake has been made by a different group of children, then hold a circle time for all the children to share and compare their work. Ask individual children to describe how they made their snakes. What do they like/dislike about them?

Encourage the children to decide whether they think their snake wiggles well or not and to tell you why.

Support
Concentrate on making just two different types of snakes for the children to compare. Provide plenty of adult help.

Extension
Challenge the children to make at least two types of snakes each, and ask them to discuss the advantages and disadvantages of each one.

Learning objectives
To build and construct with a wide range of objects; to select the tools and techniques needed to shape, assemble and join materials.

Group size
Small groups.

Home links
Invite parents and carers to come in and help with the different activities. Encourage regular help for designing and making tasks.

Learning objective
To build and construct with a wide range of objects, selecting appropriate resources and adapting work where necessary.

Group size
Small groups.

Home links
Let the children take home their decorated eggs as Easter gifts (you may have to request that the children return the boxes that were made from construction equipment!).

A nest egg

What you need
A hard-boiled egg for each child; egg cups or sections of card egg-boxes; poster paints or felt-tipped pens; paintbrushes; card; paper; construction toys such as Lego or Sticklebricks; a selection of junk materials including boxes, shredded paper, cotton wool, tissue and fabric scraps; glue; sticky tape; scissors.

Preparation
Hard-boil an egg for each child and allow the eggs to cool.

What to do
Work with small groups of children at a time and give each child a hard-boiled egg held steady in an eggcup. Explain that you would like them to carefully decorate their egg with patterns and pictures of their choice. Provide the children with poster paints and paintbrushes or felt-tipped pens and allow them to decorate their eggs in their own way. Emphasize that they must not press too hard when doing this, so as not to crack the shells. Show them how to turn their eggs carefully once they are dry, so that they can paint the under-sides as well.

Once the eggs are completely dry, explain to the children that they may take their egg home, but they need to make a container to keep it safe. Invite the children to choose from your selection of junk materials and construction toys and ask them to tell you how they will make their container before they begin. As they work, encourage them to modify their ideas when necessary and to experiment with the different materials until they are satisfied. To make sure that the eggs do not roll around and get damaged inside the box, challenge the children to choose some of the materials to pad the container carefully.

Before home-time, encourage the children to show the group their eggs and containers, explaining how they made them.

Support
Provide the children with ready-made containers and suggest that they think of ways to pad the container to stop the eggs from rolling around inside them.

Extension
Encourage the children to make their own boxes from card rather than selecting ready-made ones from the selection of junk materials.

Parting the sea

What you need

A version of the story of Pesach (Passover) such as a children's bible version or the story in *Spring and Summer Festivals* by Carole Court (*Themes for Early Years* series, Scholastic); three pieces of paper – two

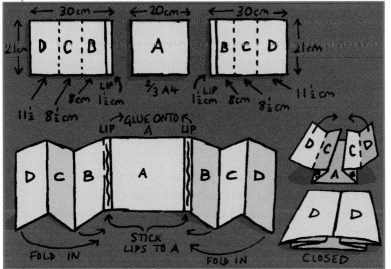

A4 and one two-thirds – A4 for each child; paints; paintbrushes; colouring materials; sticky tape or glue sticks.

What to do

Read a simplified version of the Pesach story. Concentrate on the theme of freedom and how Moses parted the sea to lead his people to the Promised Land. Discuss the word 'freedom'. Try to explain it in ways the children will understand, such as the difference between people living in prisons and people living in their own homes.

Explain that you are going to make a special picture of the sea being parted. Working with small groups at a time, give each child the two pieces of A4 paper. Show them how to fold each piece, concertina style, into thirds with a 'lip' folded at one edge. Ask them to unfold each piece of paper and paint both sides of each piece to look like the waves of the sea. Leave these pieces to dry.

Now give each child the third piece of paper and talk about what the

'Promised Land' might look like. Listen to the children's ideas, then encourage them to draw or paint a picture of the Promised Land onto this piece of paper.

Finally, help each child to refold their two 'waves' pictures and attach the 'lip' folded edges with sticky tape or a small amount of glue to either side of their Promised Land picture so that the waves completely cover the picture underneath. Show them to unfold the waves to simulate the parting of the sea in the Pesach story.

Support

Fold the paper for the children and fix the parting waves in place for them.

Extension

Invite the children to retell the story to you. Scribe their words on the back of their pictures.

Leader of the day

What you need
The photocopiable sheet on page 67;
stickers or a plain badge that can be
decorated; colouring materials.

Preparation
Familiarize yourself with the story of
how Guru Gobind Singh chose five men
to be his soldiers to protect the weak.

What to do
Tell the children the story on the
photocopiable sheet of how Guru
Gobind Singh selected five worthy men
to be his soldiers. Explain that it was
the soldiers' job to protect the weak
and needy. The soldiers all wore a
special uniform that identified them,
and today Sikh men still wear a sort of
uniform as a sign of their beliefs.

Now focus on the concept of having
a leader – Guru Gobind Singh was a
leader. Tell the children that you would
like them all to take a turn at being the
'leader of the day'. Explain that each
day the leader will wear a special
badge (a sort of uniform) to show who
they are. The leader will have special
jobs to do such as being at the front of
the line, feeding the group pet,
watering the plants, running important
errands and, most importantly, looking
after any child who is feeling left out or
who is upset or poorly in some way.
The leader will be similar to one of
Guru Gobind Singh's soldiers who
helped to look after the poor and the
weak. Ensure you establish the 'leader
of the day' as a regular part of your
group's routine.

Support
Tell the children an abridged version of
the story and concentrate on the
concept of leadership and looking after
the needy.

Extension
Encourage the children to help you
brainstorm a list of the leader's duties.
Ask them to design a special uniform
for the leader of the group.

Flower festival

Learning objectives
To begin to know about own cultures and beliefs and those of others; to find out about and identify some features of living things that they observe.

Group size
Whole group for discussion; small groups for activity.

What you need
A book about Hanamatsuri such as *The Birth of Buddha* by Judith Evans-Lowndes and W Owen Cole (*Heinemann Stories from World Religion* series, Heinemann); vases; card for labels; tissue paper; crêpe paper; paints; paper.

Preparation
Read a book about Hanamatsuri such as *The Birth of Buddha* as useful background information. Send a letter home to parents and carers asking if their child could bring in a flower or two from their gardens.

What to do
Tell the children about the Japanese flower festival, Hanamatsuri, which celebrates the Buddha's birthday. Explain that pictures of the infant Buddha are placed on small stands that are decorated with flowers as a reminder of the garden in which the Buddha was born. Children pour perfumed tea over the statues of Buddha as a reminder of the perfumed water provided by heavenly spirits for his first bath.

Place all the children's flowers that they have brought from home in a temporary display and work with small groups at a time to sort the flowers by different criteria such as size, colour, shape, number of petals and so on. Name the different flowers and write these on pieces of card. Point out the different parts of the flowers such as petal, leaf and stalk.

Continue the flower festival theme throughout the day by making tissue- and crêpe-paper flowers and making paintings and observational drawings of the real flowers.

Support
Sort the flowers by simple criteria only, such as colour and size.

Extension
Follow up the activity with a visit to a local park or gardens to see the spring flower displays.

Home links
Invite parents and carers to come in and see the children's flower festival display. Let each child present their parents or carers with a posy to take home.

Days gone by

What you need
May Day artefacts such as information and archive photographs from your local library or museum service, anecdotes and photographs from members of the local community, information books about festivals, customs and traditions; long colourful ribbons; cardboard tube; sticky coloured paper; the photocopiable sheet on page 68.

Preparation
Make a table display of the artefacts and books and adorn it with ribbons and a maypole made from a cardboard tube covered in sticky coloured paper with ribbons attached. Make an enlarged copy of the photocopiable sheet.

What to do
Draw the children's attention to the table display and show them a selection of the pictures and books. Give them some time to explore the artefacts for themselves.

Now talk to the children about the traditions of the festival of May Day – such as decorating a tree or maypole, ribbon dancing, floral garlands and May queens. Show them an enlarged copy of the photocopiable sheet and talk about what it shows. Do they think the picture shows a modern scene or does it show an event in the past? What are the people in the picture doing?

Invite the children to talk about their own experiences such as processions and parades that they may have seen or been involved in. Can they remember what they were celebrating and when it was? Did they see people in costumes, or dress up in costumes themselves? Was there dancing or singing or music playing? Can they tell you about the similarities and differences between their parade or procession and the one in the picture?

Finish the session by doing some circle singing and dancing. Give the children ribbons to wave and ask them to make a circle and move slowly around as they sing some of their favourite songs such as 'Here We Go Round the Mulberry Bush' (adapted with the words 'Here We Go Round the May Day Ring').

Support
Work with small groups of children and give each child a copy of the photocopiable sheet to colour as you encourage them to tell you about their own experiences of fêtes, festivals and processions.

Extension
Provide the children with a selection of junk materials, ribbons and paper and encourage them to make their own mini maypole.

Summer mobiles

What you need
Two lengths (30cm each) of bamboo or dowelling rod for each child; string; scissors; card; paper; paints or colouring materials; information books about summer and summer activities; collage materials; glue; sticky tape; stapler; piece of rope or washing line and pegs.

Preparation
Use the string to tie each pair of dowelling rods or bamboo canes in a 'cross' shape. Tie a piece of string (30cm long) to each of the four ends and another piece to the centre (20cm long) ready for hanging up.

What to do
Ask the children to think about summer-time. What is the weather generally like? What things do the children wear? Do they do any special activities? Are they able to play outside sometimes – what games do they play? Do they eat any special foods? What are their favourite summer foods?

Explain to the children that they are going to make a summer mobile. Show them the bamboo or dowelling crosses and tell them that they need to add four items relating to summer – one for each corner – to their mobiles. Look together at some information books about summer and summer activities and brainstorm a list of suggestions for summer objects that the children could make. Ideas could include buckets and spades, sun-hats, sunflowers and ice-creams.

Encourage the children to choose their first object and to draw it onto a piece of card. Invite them to paint, colour or add collage materials to their drawings, and then help them to cut out the shapes and attach them to one of the pieces of string on the mobile. Repeat the process with the other three objects.

String a piece of rope or washing line across your room and suspend the children's finished summer mobiles with pegs.

Support
Work with four children at a time and make a group mobile, with each child making one summer object. Help the group to cut out and fix their objects to the mobile.

Extension
Invite the children to use junk materials to make three-dimensional objects to hang onto the mobiles.

Learning objectives
To use a wide range of objects to make a mobile; to select the tools and techniques needed to shape, assemble and join the materials that they are using.

Group size
Small groups.

Home links
Invite the children to bring in summer objects such as sun-hats, buckets and spades and clean, empty ice-cream tubs from home to use for a table-top summer display.

Holiday time

What you need
A selection of your own holiday photographs, postcards, holiday brochures and souvenirs; the children's own holiday souvenirs and photographs showing past summer holidays and outings; a display area covered with blue or yellow backing paper; paper; pencils; colouring materials.

Preparation
Send a letter home or put up a notice explaining to parents and carers that you are going to be doing some work on the children's past summer holidays and outings. Ask parents and carers if they would let their children bring in photographs, postcards or souvenirs from their holidays and outings to show to the rest of the group.

What to do
Show the children your selection of holiday souvenirs, postcards and photographs, telling them a little bit about each one. Encourage them to listen carefully and explain that you will be asking them to share their souvenirs afterwards. Invite them to ask you some questions about your summer holidays or outings.

Now invite the children, in turn, to come to the front of the group with their holiday photos or souvenirs. Encourage them to show them to the rest of the group and to tell the other children a little bit about their souvenir or photograph and their holiday or outing. Ask each child one or two questions and encourage the other children to think of some questions to ask, too. Make sure that all the children are given a chance to show and talk about their souvenirs.

Now give each child a piece of paper, a pencil and colouring materials. Ask them to draw a picture about their holiday or outing. Encourage them to tell you about their picture and write down some of their memories and comments. Make a display of the children's photographs, souvenirs and drawings, and label them with some of the children's comments and memories.

Support
Give the children more confidence to talk about their souvenirs by working with small groups at a time.

Extension
Provide the children with blank postcards and ask them to imagine that they are back on their holiday or outing. Encourage them to draw a picture of the place and ask them to write a message on the back and send their cards to their families.

Summer fête

What you need
The book *Dogger* by Shirley Hughes (Red Fox); junk materials; scissors; glue; small games equipment; counting equipment; construction toys; one adult helper per group.

What to do
Read *Dogger* to the children. Talk about the story together and remind them of the summer fête in the story. Look at the picture of the fête. What can the children see? Have they ever been to a summer fête? What sort of games and stalls did they see there?

Explain to the children that you are going to hold a mini summer fête and that you would like their help to make up the games.

Divide the children into small groups or pairs. Allocate a group of children to an adult helper and provide them with a selection of small games equipment such as bats, balls, quoits and beanbags. Encourage the children to work with a partner to try to make up a simple game to play with the equipment.

Work with another group of children and provide them with a selection of junk and collage materials. Include tubes, lids, tubs and boxes in the selection and help the children to devise some games using the equipment. Let the children use other resources to develop their ideas. For example, they could create a game that involves throwing Unifix cubes into a yoghurt pot, or a game that requires the use of a dice.

Make sure that all the children have been involved in at least one of the two activities and then encourage individuals to demonstrate how their games work to the rest of the group. At a later session, invite some extra adult helpers and set up a selection of the games for the children to try out at a mini summer fête!

Support
Give the children lots of practical suggestions to help them devise a game. Let them work with an adult helper if they find it too difficult to work with a partner.

Extension
Encourage the children to make up more sophisticated games and suggest that they write down or tell you the rules of their game.

Learning objectives
To build and construct with a wide range of objects, selecting appropriate resources; to select the tools and techniques needed to shape, assemble and join the materials.

Group size
Whole group for discussion and story; small groups for activity.

Home links
Invite parents and carers to come in and supervise the games at your mini summer fête!

Keeping cool

What you need
An enlarged copy of the photocopiable sheet on page 69; board; large pieces of fabric; sun-hats; suncream; sun umbrellas; cool drinks.

What to do
Talk to the children about hot and sunny weather. What sort of clothes do they wear when it is hot? What clothes help them to keep cool? Can the

any of these ways? Invite them to talk about their experiences. Look at the picture of the sun umbrella with the children and explain how it provides shade from the sun.

On a hot and sunny day, take the children into your outside area and ask them to look for shady spots. Can they see what objects or living things are creating the shade? Perhaps it is a building or a tree. Draw the children's attention to their own shadows and explain that they are making shady areas, too!

Give groups or pairs of children some sun umbrellas and pieces of fabric and invite them to drape these between posts, fences, chairs and so on to create a few shady spots in your outside area. Use this opportunity to talk to the children about the importance of covering up in the sun and provide them with sun-hats and protective suncream.

Once the children have created some shady spots, encourage them to sit in one and provide cool drinks to help them to really cool down!

Support
Some children may find it hard to fully appreciate the concept of shade and shadows. Help them to experience and describe the difference between standing in the shade and standing in the sunshine.

Extension
Provide the children with their own copy of the photocopiable sheet and ask them to cut out the pictures and paste each one onto a separate piece of paper. Encourage each child to write a sentence about keeping cool under the individual pictures.

Finally, staple the pages together to make a book and let the children enjoy reading it together.

children think of any other ways of keeping cool? Make a list of their ideas on the board.

Show the children the enlarged copy of the photocopiable sheet. Ask them to look carefully at the pictures and encourage them to discuss how each of the objects help to keep people cool when it is hot. Have the children tried

Beach huts

Learning objective
To build and construct with a wide range of objects, selecting appropriate resources and adapting work where necessary.

Group size
Four to six children.

What you need
Pictures and information books about the seaside, including images of traditional beach huts; sand tray; small-world people; selection of junk materials; construction toys such as Lego; collage materials; scissors; glue; sticky tape; paints.

Preparation
Gather a selection of junk and collage materials that are suitable for making model beach huts and the furniture to go inside them.

What to do
Show the children a selection of pictures and information books about the seaside. Encourage them to join in with the discussion by contributing their own experiences or knowledge of the seaside. Show pictures of beach huts and explain to the children what they are used for. What sort of things do they think they would find inside the huts? If they had a beach hut, what would they put inside it?

Provide the children with a selection of junk materials and together, discuss ways of using them to make a beach hut. Ask questions that will help them to consider the materials and resources they will need, such as 'How will you fix the roof to the sides of the building?', 'What will you use to make a door?' and so on. Encourage the children to keep their designs simple and help them when necessary. Once they have painted or decorated their huts, help them to use collage, junk and construction materials to make objects to go inside.

Let the children play with their finished huts in the sand tray, using small-world people to help act out their seaside stories.

Support
Let the children decorate small boxes in bright colours to make their beach huts. Encourage them to use construction toys to make simple furniture to go inside their huts.

Extension
Invite the children to make other seaside buildings such as a café, ice-cream parlour and shop.

Home links
Suggest to parents and carers that they let their children use junk materials to make similar models of their own homes or bedrooms. Invite the children to bring in any models they have made to show the rest of the group.

A perfect place

What you need
Board or easel; sugar paper; pen; colouring and drawing materials; small-world toys and people.

What to do
Brainstorm a list of the places that the children have been to. Did they go to these places for holidays, outings or to see people? What places did they like the most and why? Ask them to describe the different places, prompting them with questions if necessary.

Now ask the children to think about the type of summer holiday place that they would like to go to if they could choose anywhere. Would it have a beach? Would there be some woods for walking in? Would it have paths to ride bicycles on? Would there be a park to play in? Write down all the children's ideas on a board or easel.

Provide a large piece of sugar paper and explain that you would like the children to help you draw a map of their ideal holiday place on the paper. Choose one of the ideas from your list and show the children how to draw a plan version of it onto the paper. Let each child choose a feature and help them to draw it, in pencil first, onto the paper. When the map is complete, and the paper is full, remind the children what each part of the map shows. Now let the children colour the map, and provide them with small-world toys and people. Encourage pairs of children to use the map as a playmat for some imaginative small-world play.

Support
Work with pairs or individual children and draw each suggestion that they make onto the paper for them. Concentrate on encouraging them to use and develop the appropriate geographical vocabulary. Support their imaginative play by suggesting scenarios and by inviting them to act out episodes from their own experiences, such as a visit to the park or seaside.

Extension
Provide the children with some junk or construction materials and suggest that they make some models to use with the map.

Lights and lanterns

What you need
Pictures of different festivals showing lights, such as Wesak showing lanterns and candles in temples or homes, Christmas tree lights, diva lamps,

Hanukkah candles and so on; a copy of the photocopiable sheet on page 70 for each child and one enlarged copy; colouring materials; pencils.

Preparation
Before carrying out this activity, it will be helpful for the children to have some knowledge of other festivals that use lights, lanterns and so on as part of the celebrations and symbolism.

What to do
Explain to the children that the festival of Wesak is when Buddhists remember Buddha's birth, enlightenment and death by giving gifts to the poor and

by decorating their temples and homes with lanterns, candles and flowers. There are processions held in the temples with people carrying candles and burning incense sticks.

Talk to the children about how 'light' is a feature of many important festivals. Can the children think of any examples, such as candles and lights for Christmas trees, diva lamps for Divali and so on? Talk about the different festivals and how they are celebrated using lights and lanterns in a variety of ways.

Show the children an enlarged copy of the photocopiable sheet and talk about the different types of light shown. Which ones do the children recognize? Discuss how some of the lights are made using electricity and how some are made from candles or flames. Give each child a copy of the photocopiable sheet and let them colour the objects. Encourage them to write the name (or first letter) of the object underneath each one, scribing for them if necessary.

Support
Talk to the children about the different types of light they can see on the photocopiable sheet and invite them to tell you about just one of the objects.

Extension
Encourage the children to tell you a little bit about each light source shown on the photocopiable sheet – where might they see each object and what might it be used for?

Making a mark

What you need
Examples of engraved objects such as trophies, jewellery, coins, pictures of monuments; Plasticine; Plasticine tools suitable for making marks and writing with; examples of different types of writing such as pictures of old and illuminated manuscripts, handwriting, computer writing and so on.

Preparation
Set up a table with Plasticine and tools and collect some examples of engraved and other types of writing (see above).

What to do
Tell the children that the Jewish festival of Shavuot celebrates the time when Moses found out about the Ten Commandments (special rules) while he was on a mountain called Mount Sinai. Explain to the children that Moses wrote these special rules down on tablets (pieces) of stone.

Look at some examples of engraving with the children, such as on trophies, monuments, coins, plates and jewellery. Tell them that they will be doing some 'engraving' of their own using Plasticine and tools.

Give each child a large piece of Plasticine and show them how to shape it into a 'tablet of stone'. Provide them with tools and suggest that they make some marks on their tablet, such as the numbers from 1 to10 or their name.

Conclude by looking at and comparing a variety of different styles of writing, such as those found in old manuscripts, illuminated scripts, modern computer writing, handwriting and so on.

Support
Let the children enjoy making marks and play-writing on the Plasticine 'tablets' with their tools.

Extension
Encourage the children to think of a special rule to inscribe on their 'tablet'.

Processions and parades

What you need
Ingredients for sandwiches and fruit squash; cardboard tubes; orange crêpe paper; scissors; glue sticks; sticky tape; paints; colouring materials; card; dowelling rods; sugar paper; collage materials; adult helpers.

Preparation
Set up four tables, with an adult helper at each table, to include the following:
◆ ingredients for making simple sandwiches and fruit squash
◆ cardboard tubes and orange crêpe paper for making pretend torches – the children can decorate the tubes using paints or colouring materials and then cut out and scrunch up some crêpe paper to make a flame for their torch
◆ sugar paper, dowelling rods, colouring and collage materials for making flags – the children can cut out a flag shape from the sugar paper and decorate it in the style of their choice, then attach their pennants to the dowelling rods to make flags
◆ card, dowelling rods, collage and colouring materials for making stick puppets – the children can cut out a card shape of their choice (perhaps a person or animal), decorate it and attach it to a piece of dowelling to make a stick puppet.

What to do
Explain to the children that Midsummer's Day (24 June) comes shortly after the longest day of the year (21 June), when we have the most daylight, and that traditional Midsummer celebrations include bonfires, feasts, torchlit processions, parades and fancy dress.

Tell the children that you are going to have your own Midsummer celebration with a feast and a procession around your setting. Explain that they will each have a turn at making something to eat for the feast and something to carry and wave for the procession.

Divide the children into four groups and allocate each group to one of the tables that you have prepared. Ensure that all the children have a chance to make something to eat and something to wave!

At the end of the session, hold your mini feast and then process around your group setting, waving puppets,

flags or torches to some suitable music, such as Vivaldi's 'Summer' from *The Four Seasons*.

Support
Set up two tables only – one for making sandwiches and the other for making flags.

Extension
Challenge the children to make colourful summer hats to wear for the Midsummer procession.

Learning objective
To select the tools and techniques they need to shape, assemble and join the materials.

Group size
Four small groups.

Home links
Invite parents and carers to join you for the feast. Ask for extra adult help on the day.

Special memories

What you need
Paper; pencils; colouring materials;
envelopes.

Preparation
Discuss Father's Day sensitively with the
children so as to include children from
all different family backgrounds.
Explain to the
children that they
may send cards and
gifts to any special
male person on this
day, such as a
grandfather, older
brother, uncle or
family friend.

What to do
Gather the children
together and invite
them to close their
eyes and think
carefully about their
families and friends,
in particular their
fathers, brothers,
grandfathers, uncles
and male carers.
Explain that Father's
Day is a time to pay
special attention to
men that play an
important role in
their lives.

about their special memory. Give them
a piece of paper, pencil and colouring
materials and ask them to fill the page
with a picture that shows their special
memory. As each child finishes their
picture, ask them to tell you what the
picture shows. Scribe their words onto
the back of the picture. Provide the

   Ask the children to try and
remember something special that they
have done with their fathers. Help them
to think of ideas such as an outing to a
park, being read a story, playing a
game, playing in the garden and so on.
When the children have thought of
their special memory, encourage them
to share it with the rest of the group.
Ensure that all the children have a
chance to talk about their memories.
   Now work with small groups of
children and begin by asking each child

children with envelopes to put their
pictures in and let them take them
home to give as gifts on Father's Day.

Support
Work with small groups only and limit
the discussion time to allow for shorter
concentration spans.

Extension
Encourage the children to write or tell
you a special Father's Day message to
include on the back of the picture.

Shape biscuits

What you need
A basic biscuit recipe and ingredients; a cooker (for adult use only); plastic pastry shape cutters; plastic cutlery and so on.

Preparation
Discuss Father's Day sensitively with the children so as to include children from all different family backgrounds. Explain to the children that they may send cards and gifts to any special male person on this day such as a grandfather, older brother, uncle or family friend.

What to do
Explain to the children that they are going to make some special shape biscuits for Father's Day. Ask them to think about the things that their fathers or male carers like doing such as watching or playing football, reading, gardening, driving, cooking and so on. Encourage the children to think of shapes that they could make their biscuits into that would match their fathers' hobbies.

Find a simple biscuit recipe (most good children's cookery books will include one) and work with small groups at a time to make some biscuit dough. Give each child a piece of dough (enough to make two or three biscuits each) and provide them with a selection of shape cutters and plastic tools such as plastic cutlery, clean lids and so on. Help each child to decide on the shape that they are going to make and show them how to use the different tools.

Bake the biscuits and draw the children's attention to how the biscuit dough has changed in the oven. Let the children take the biscuits home to give as a Father's Day gift.

Support
Help the children to cut out the biscuit shapes and let them use shape cutters rather than tools for the basic shapes. Encourage them to use the tools for making patterns on their biscuits.

Extension
Suggest that the children make special envelopes or gift boxes to put their biscuits in.

Learning objectives
To look closely at how things change; to use tools to shape materials.

Group size
Small groups.

Home links
Invite parents and carers to come into your setting on a regular basis to do some cookery or craft activities with the children.

The best boat

What you need
A table set out with silver foil, balsa wood, Plasticine, pieces of Polystyrene, scissors, glue, sticky tape, small tacks, child's hammer, paper; water tray.

What to do
Tell the children about the Chinese Dragon Boat Festival. The festival honours Ch'u Yuan, a statesman and poet who drowned himself in protest at the Emperor of the time. His followers rushed after him to save his body from being eaten by the fish. Today, dragon boat races are held to symbolize the rush to save him.

Explain to the children that they are going to make some small model boats to use in the water tray. Ask them to think about what makes a good boat. For example, does it need to be strong, fast or steady?

Work with small groups of children at a time and examine the different materials that you have set out on the table. Encourage the children to describe the different properties of the materials. Do they think they will float or sink? How do they think they will fix them together to make a boat? What

other materials will they need? (Glue, paste, small nails and so on.) Do the children have any ideas for how they are going to make their boats?

Once the children have chosen their materials, help them to assemble simple boat shapes and allow them to try them out in the water tray. Encourage them to modify their designs as they go along so that they are sturdier.

Support
Provide just one type of material such as the silver foil and show the children how to carefully shape it to make a simple boat shape. Let them place one or two small-world people into their boats and encourage the children to use them for imaginative play in the water tray.

Extension
Invite the children to test out the strength and suitability of their boats. For example, they could test them to see how many small-world people they will hold and then race the boats by blowing them across the water tray using straws.

Keeping dry

What you need
Display table and board; blue backing paper; rain-themed border; paper; the photocopiable sheet on page 71; umbrellas; raincoats; Wellington boots; rainhats; pencils; paints; paintbrushes; marker pen.

Preparation
Cover the display board in blue backing paper and add a rain-themed border such as raindrops, rainbows or umbrellas. Set up a display table beneath the board and place the rain gear on the table. Copy the rhyme 'Rain on the green grass' from the photocopiable sheet onto a large piece of paper and place in the centre of the display board.

What to do
Tell the children about the legend of St Swithun's Day. Explain that it is said that if it rains on St Swithun's Day, then it is likely to be wet for the next 40 days! Invite the children to help you to brainstorm a list of ways to keep dry in the rain. Show them the objects on the table and ask individual children to model them. Ask the children to describe what each object is made of and how it is used to keep out the rain. What would happen if the objects were made of other materials such as paper or cardboard? Would they still be good at keeping out the rain? Make a note of the children's descriptions and use their words to make captions for the display.

Give each child a piece of paper, paints and a paintbrush. Invite them to draw a picture of themselves in their rainy-day clothes. Add the children's pictures to the display board.

Enlarge the photocopiable sheet to A3 size and read the traditional rhymes to the children. Learn them together and encourage the children to develop some actions to go with the words.

Support
Help the children to describe the materials that the rain gear is made from. Introduce words such as shiny, soft and slippery.

Extension
Work with groups of children to make an illustrated book of rainy-day rhymes. Ask the children to cut out and illustrate the rhymes from the photocopiable sheet. Include other nursery favourites such as 'Incy Wincy Spider', 'I Hear Thunder' and 'Pitter, Patter, Pit, Pat'.

Caring for others

What you need
Paper; pencils; colouring materials; a story-book about caring for others such as *Can't You Sleep, Little Bear?* or *You and Me, Little Bear* both by Martin Waddell and illustrated by Barbara Firth (Walker Books).

What to do
Talk to the children about the Hindu festival of Raksha Bandhan and explain that it is a time when Hindus think about caring for their families. During the festival, girls tie special thread bracelets called 'rakhis' around their brothers' wrists to give them strength. In return, the brothers promise to protect their sisters.

Read *Can't You Sleep, Little Bear?* or *You and Me, Little Bear* to the children. Talk about how Big Bear looks after and protects Little Bear. Encourage the children to try and remember a time when they protected or looked after someone, or how they themselves were looked after by someone (such as a brother, sister or friend). Invite them to share their memories with the rest of

the group. Ask the children to listen to each other carefully.

Now give each child a piece of paper, pencil and colouring materials and ask them to draw a picture to show how they cared for, or were cared for by, someone. Encourage each child to tell you about their picture and scribe a caption for them underneath their drawing. Make a display of the children's pictures, explaining the link between their work and the festival of Raksha Bandhan.

Support
If the children are unable to remember an event to draw, let them draw a picture from the story that they have just heard. Remind them of how the festival of Raksha Bandhan is about caring for others.

Extension
Provide older children with some thin ribbons and show them how to tie the ends together and then twist and intertwine them to make a simple rakhi bracelet. Let them glue fabric shapes to their rakhis and allow them to take them home to give to someone special.

Helping squirrel

What you need
Information or picture books about autumn; paper; pencils; colouring materials.

Preparation
Share some information and picture books about autumn with the children. If possible, draw their attention to pictures of animals and their autumnal activities.

What to do
Have a general discussion about autumn with the children. Explain that it is a busy time for many animals who are working hard to get ready for the winter. Tell them that during autumn, squirrels are usually very busy hiding nuts and acorns which they will eat later in the year when there is not much food around for them.

Ask the children to think about where squirrels live. Have any of the children seen a squirrel in their garden or at the local park? Where might a squirrel choose to hide his nuts and acorns? Explain that sometimes squirrels can't remember all the places that they have hidden their food.

Work with small groups of children and provide each child with a piece of paper and some drawing and colouring materials. Tell them that they are going to draw a map to show where a squirrel lives and where it has hidden its nuts

and acorns. Ask each child to decide where their squirrel lives and encourage them to make a detailed drawing of that place. Suggest ideas to make their drawings as full and interesting as possible. For example, if they have chosen a park, perhaps there is a pond and a bench there, as well as trees, hedges and grass.

Once the children have completed their pictures, encourage them to think

about where a squirrel might hide his food. Ask them to draw an acorn or a nut in each hiding place.

Support
Draw a simple garden or parkland scene and ask the children to draw acorns or nuts where they think the squirrel might hide them.

Extension
Make lift-the-flap pictures with the children and encourage them to draw, using coloured pencils, their hidden nuts or acorns under the flaps.

Learning objective
To find out about and identify some features of living things and the natural world.

Group size
Whole group for discussion; small groups for activity.

Home links
Invite parents and carers to accompany the group on an autumn walk to look for squirrels and other wildlife as they prepare for the winter.

Autumn colours

What you need
Adult helpers; coloured pencils or crayons; a clipboard and piece of paper for each child; enlarged copy of the photocopiable sheet on page 72; autumn-coloured paints; palettes.

Preparation
Send a letter home with the children explaining that they are going to go on a local walk and ask for the parents' permission. Invite parents and carers to

volunteer to accompany the group. Choose a route for your walk that will allow the children to see a range of autumn colours.

What to do
Explain to the children that you will be taking them on an autumn walk in the local area to look for all the changes that happen during the autumn. Tell

them that you would like them to look at the colours of all the natural things that they see.

Divide your children into small groups and allocate an adult helper to each group (check your Local Education Authority's guidelines for the adult-to-child ratio). Give each group a set of coloured pencils or crayons and each child a piece of paper attached to a clipboard. While you are on your walk, ask the children to stop regularly and look at the colours of the trees, hedges and plants. Suggest that they use the coloured pencils or crayons to record the range of colours that they see.

Back at your setting, read the poem on the photocopiable sheet to the children. Does the poem remind them of the walk? Discuss the colours that they saw and share some of the children's observations.

Divide the children back into their small groups and explain that they are going to use the colour observations that they made on their walk to do some autumn colour-mixing using paints. Provide paper, paint palettes and a selection of paints and help the children to mix up the autumn colours that they noticed on their walk.

Use an enlarged copy of the poem as a focus for a stimulus display. Place the children's autumn colour-mixing work around the poem and caption it with the children's comments and observations from the walk.

Support
Help the children to mix just one of the autumn colours that they noticed on the walk.

Extension
Encourage the children to make more detailed field sketches, including leaf shapes as well as colours that they noticed on the walk.

○ Leaf models

What you need
Leaves brought in by the children; a large tray; a copy of the photocopiable sheet on page 73 stuck onto card; scissors; Plasticine or clay; Plasticine tools such as rolling pins, spatulas, plastic knives and so on; paints; paper.

Preparation
Ask the children to bring in a few different-shaped and different-coloured leaves that have fallen in their gardens or close to their home.

What to do
At circle time, let the children show the leaves they have collected. Encourage them to describe the shape and appearance of their leaves as they show them to the rest of the group. Collect all the leaves together in a big tray and put it in the middle of a table.

Work with small groups of children at a time and ask them to help you sort out the leaves. Look closely at each one and discuss the colour, shape and appearance. Compare the different leaves – what are their similarities and differences? With the children's help, decide how you will sort them, for example, by colour, by size or into sets

of rounded and pointy leaves. Show the children the photocopiable sheet and ask them to try and match some of their leaves to the illustrations. Then cut out the individual leaf shapes from the photocopiable sheet and lay them out in front of the children.

Provide each child with a lump of Plasticine or clay and ask them to roll it out flat. Suggest that they lay the leaf templates on top of the Plasticine and cut around the shapes using plastic tools. Encourage them to use other tools to make vein patterns on top of them. If using clay, let the children paint their leaf shapes once they are dry. Alternatively, use the dried clay or Plasticine leaves to make some leaf prints by dipping them into paint and pressing them down gently onto paper.

Support
Look at a smaller selection of leaves with the children and provide a choice of two simple shapes to mould with the Plasticine.

Extension
Ask the children to make their own leaf shapes in clay or Plasticine, rather than using the card templates.

Learning objectives
To look closely at similarities, differences and patterns; to observe and find out about the natural world.

Group size
Whole group for discussion; small groups for activity.

Home links
Suggest that parents and carers do some autumn leaf rubbings with their children by placing a leaf under a piece of paper and rubbing over it with an appropriately coloured crayon.

Collect the leaves

What you need
A wide selection of junk materials including card, tubes, corrugated card, boxes and pots; glue; sticky tape; stapler; split-pin fasteners; paints; paintbrushes; paper; scissors.

Preparation
Set out the junk materials and equipment on a large table.

What to do
Have a general discussion with the children about autumn time. Remind them of some of the special characteristics of autumn such as leaves falling, conkers ripening and falling from the trees, animals working hard to store their winter food supplies and so on.

Explain that you have set up an 'inventor's table' and that you are going to ask a few children at a time to try to make some useful autumn machines or objects to make autumn jobs easier. What do the children understand by the word 'machine'? What sort of machines do they think would be useful to have in the autumn? If the children find it hard to think of any, offer suggestions such as a machine to collect leaves, a special box to store conkers, or a digger for squirrels to use to bury their acorns!

Work with small groups of children at a time and ask each group to decide firstly on the type of machine that they

are going to make. Once they have decided, ask them to think about what they need to make it. Can they find the materials they need on the table? Are there any materials that might work better than others?

Once the children have a plan as to how they will make their models, help them to try out different ways of fixing their materials together. Let them paint or decorate their finished models. Finally, encourage them to share their models at circle time, and make a display of their finished work.

Support
Limit the amount of materials for the children to choose from and suggest a simple task such as making a conker storage box. Help them to select and fix their materials together.

Extension
Suggest that the children draw a plan of their 'invention' before they begin. Encourage them to adapt and evaluate their designs as they work.

Preparing for winter

What you need
Outdoor toys and equipment; cleaning materials; dressing-up clothes; paper; pencils; colouring materials.

What to do
Ask the children if they can remember all the changes that happen during autumn time. Together, talk about how the leaves start to fall and how the days get shorter and darker. Can they remember any of the things that some animals do during the autumn to get ready for the winter? Talk about how some animals gather and store food, how some birds such as swallows migrate and how some animals go into hibernation.

Now ask the children to consider the things that they themselves (and other people such as their families and friends) do to get ready for the winter. Invite them to share their ideas with the rest of the group. They might include putting away all their summer clothes, cleaning and storing the outdoor toys and garden furniture, getting out the bird-table to feed the winter birds and so on.

After the discussion, enlist the help of some of the children to take part in preparations for the winter such as cleaning the outdoor toys, setting up a bird-table and sorting the dressing-up clothes into winter and summer piles.

Now work with groups of children and provide each child with a piece of paper divided in half. Ask them to draw a picture of themselves getting ready for winter on one half of the page, and a picture of an animal getting ready for

winter on the other half of the page. Ask the children to tell you about their pictures and scribe captions for them.

Support
Concentrate on the practical cleaning-up and sorting activities. Encourage the children to draw a single picture of one of the ways that they have helped the

group to get ready for winter and to tell you about it.

Extension
Provide the children with small, blank zigzag books and ask each child to fill their pages with as many pictures and words as possible of the different ways that both people and animals get ready for the winter.

Learning objective
To find out about and identify some features of events they observe.

Group size
Whole group for discussion; small groups for activity.

Home links
Encourage parents and carers to discuss with their children the ways they prepare for winter at home. Suggest that they let their child sort their clothes into summer and winter sets.

Hibernating habits

Learning objective
To find out about and identify some features of living things.

Group size
Whole group.

What you need
Suitable music such as JS Bach's *Sheep May Safely Graze* (available on many classical compilations); junk materials including boxes and tubes; twigs; leaves; mosses; scissors; glue; sticky tape.

What to do
Remind the children of all the changes that happen during the autumn and discuss how some animals hibernate during the winter. Explain that

hibernating animals prepare their homes during the autumn and that hedgehogs are one of the British mammals that do this.

Tell the children that hedgehogs make themselves cosy dens in sheltered places, for example, under boxes and sheds, under piles of twigs and leaves (such as those in bonfire piles) and in places such as unused drainpipes. Hedgehogs drag leaves, twigs, mosses and so on to their chosen spot and then make cosy nests. They curl themselves up tightly into a ball inside their nests and this helps to keep them warm.

Clear an open space and tell the children that you would like them to move like hedgehogs as they get ready for their winter hibernation. Remind them of the way that hedgehogs search for a site, gather their nesting material, make their nests and then curl up tightly to sleep. Practise each type of movement first, then play some suitable music, such as Bach's *Sheep May Safely Graze*. Encourage the children to mime the hedgehog's hibernation sequence to the music.

Follow the movement activity with some practical work. Provide the children with a selection of junk and natural materials such as tubes, boxes, fallen leaves, twigs and mosses, and challenge them to make a hedgehog's hibernation home.

Support
Keep the movement aspect as simple as possible. Concentrate on two or three types of movement and practise each one separately before linking them together to music. Move at the same time as the children to allow them to copy you and to give them extra confidence.

Extension
Find out about charities that protect hedgehogs such as The Mammal Society of Great Britain, tel: 020-74984358, and St Tiggywinkles – The Wildlife Hospital Trust, who rescue and rehabilitate all species of British wildlife, tel: 01844-292292. Discuss with the children why wild animals need protecting and how some may need to be treated if they are ill.

Home links
Encourage parents and carers to help their children to look out for the activities of birds, squirrels and other wildlife during autumn.

Drums

What you need

Two tables; a collection of drums from different parts of the world; junk materials including boxes and tubs; sticky tape; glue sticks; scissors; different types of paper including tissue, greaseproof, crêpe and sugar paper; colouring materials.

Preparation

Tell the children about the Ethiopian New Year Festival when each year in the four-year cycle is named after an evangelist. The festival is celebrated by Rastafarians on 11 September with eating, drumming and dancing. Set up a table with the collection of drums in the middle and place all the junk materials and other resources ready on a table nearby.

What to do

Pass each drum around the group, one by one. Let the children feel the materials that each one is made from, explore the sounds that each one makes and notice any patterns or adornments that the drums have. If possible, tell the children where the drums have come from.

Now show the children the selection of junk materials, paper and other resources that you prepared on the table nearby. Examine all the materials together and encourage the children to plan how they might make a drum from them.

Explain to the children that you would like them to make two simple drums, using two different types of paper to explore and compare the different sounds that they make. Help them to choose and assemble their materials. Encourage them to decorate their drum bases with patterns of their own choice or ones similar to those seen on the real drums.

Let each child in turn try out the sounds that their drums make. Compare all the different types of paper used to make the drums. Do any of them sound like the real drums?

Support

Limit the choice of paper to two types only and divide the groups in half so that both types are used. Encourage the children to make just one simple drum and provide help with fixing the paper in place and cutting the materials to size.

Extension

Listen to some traditional African or reggae music and invite the children to play the drums that they have made.

Learning objective
To investigate objects and materials using the senses as appropriate.

Group size
Small groups.

Home links
Let the children demonstrate the drums that they have made at a musical assembly. Invite parents and carers to attend and encourage them to bring along and demonstrate any instruments that they can play.

Learning objective
To find out abut past
events in the lives of
their families.

Group size
Small groups.

Memory lane

What you need
A3 card; felt-tipped pen; paper; ruler;
colouring and drawing materials;
scissors; glue sticks.

Preparation
Fold a piece of card in half so that it
stands up like a frame for each child.
Draw an oval shape in each half with a
felt-tipped pen and draw three or four
lines under each oval (see diagram).

What to do
Talk to the children about their
grandparents. Remember to be sensitive
to individual circumstances. Explain that
they are going to make simple photo
frame cards to give to their grandparents
on Grandparent's Day. Give each child a

about themselves. For example, 'I am
five and I like swimming and playing
with my brother'. Scribe their sentences
underneath their pictures.

On the reverse side of the frame,
write 'Happy Grandparent's Day' for
the children and ask them to sign their
name as they would on a greetings
card. Let the children take home the
photo frame with another piece of oval-
shaped paper stuck to the opposite
side. Send a simple note to
grandparents asking them to draw a
picture of themselves at the same age
as the child is now and to add a
sentence underneath about what they
liked to do at that age. Encourage the
children to bring the completed cards
to share with the rest of the group
before giving them back to their
grandparents.

pre-prepared frame and a piece of paper
cut to fit the oval shape. Tell the children
that you would like them to draw a
picture of their face onto the paper.
Encourage them to take their time to
draw their portraits, paying attention to
hair and eye colour and other
distinguishing features. Stick their
finished picture inside the oval on one
side of the frame. Now ask the children
individually to tell you something

Support
Provide help to the children with
choosing appropriate colours for their
portrait pictures.

Extension
Suggest that the children try to copy-
write or write their own words
underneath the picture. Encourage
them to decorate the reverse side of the
frame and to write their own personal
message to their grandparents.

Home links
Invite parents and
carers to send in
photographs of
themselves at the
same age as their
children are now with
a few words about
what they used to like
to play.

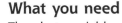
Shelters

What you need
The photocopiable sheet on page 74; a sand tray; small-world people; twigs; leaves; fabric scraps; *Sally's Secret* by Shirley Hughes (Red Fox).

Preparation
Make a copy of the photocopiable sheet for each child.

What to do
Ask the children to tell you what they think the word 'shelter' means. Can they give you any examples of a shelter? Explain that shelters are places that keep people and animals warm and dry. Think about some examples of natural shelters such as trees, caves and bushes. What animals might be found in each of these places? What other places are shelters (or homes) for animals? Ideas could include barns, kennels and baskets. Now ask the children to think about their own homes – these are shelters, too. Together, think about the other places that you find shelter in, such as friends' houses, the group setting, bus shelters and so on.

Give each child a copy of the photocopiable sheet. Ask them to talk

about the different types of shelter with you. Which ones are natural and which are made by people? Who might take shelter in each one?

Explain to the children how the Jewish people built temporary shelters when they had to escape from Egypt. Point out the picture of one of these on the photocopiable sheet. The shelters were made from leaves, twigs and other natural materials. Explain that Sukkot commemorates the Jewish people's journey and today many Jewish people make decorative sukkahs (or shelters).

Provide the children with some twigs, leaves and fabric scraps and suggest that they build a temporary shelter in the sand tray for some small-world people.

Support
Let the children build shelters from construction toys such as bricks or Lego instead of twigs and leaves.

Extension
Invite the children to use the back of the photocopiable sheet to draw at least two other types of shelter and to share ideas.

Learning objective
To find out about and identify the uses of everyday technology.

Group size
Up to four children.

Farm machines

What you need
A table; information books about farming, such as *Big Machines on the Farm* by Steve Cox (Puffin Books); small-world farm toys and vehicles; construction toys such as Lego; large piece of plain sugar paper; colouring and drawing materials; sticky tape.

Preparation
Cover a table with a large piece of plain sugar paper.

What to do
Find out what the children understand by the word 'harvest'. Expand on their understanding by explaining in simple terms what happens during a harvest. Use simple information books to show the children some pictures of farm machinery and harvesting. Together, talk about the pictures and describe the machines that can be seen. What are the machines doing? How are the crops being harvested and stored? How might the crops be harvested if there weren't any farm machines such as the ones in the pictures?

Provide the children with some colouring and drawing materials, small-world farm toys and vehicles, and construction materials such as Lego. Encourage them to decorate the sugar paper on the covered table to look like a farm with fields, hedges and so on.

Invite the children to build storage barns and a farmhouse with Lego bricks and to use the small-world toys to act out the harvesting process, using the knowledge that they have gained from the discussion.

Support
Draw a simple farm playmat for the children to colour in and use. Provide empty boxes to act as barns and the farmhouse, and encourage the children to play imaginatively with the small-world farm toys.

Extension
Provide the children with more sophisticated construction toys and challenge them to make their own farm harvesting machines.

Home links
Make a collection of farming and harvest information books and let the children borrow them to take home and share with their parents and carers.

The thick jungle

Learning objective
To find out about and identify features in the place they live and the natural world.

Group size
Whole group for discussion; small groups for activity.

What you need
The photocopiable sheet on page 75; information books showing pictures of different jungle environments; large pieces of paper; colouring and drawing materials.

What to do
Read to the children 'The story of Divali' on the photocopiable sheet, concentrating on the part of the story that tells of Rama and Sita's exile in the jungle. Ask the children to think about what a thick jungle might look like. Encourage them to share their ideas with the rest of the group. Have they read any other stories that are set in the jungle? In 'The story of Divali', we find out that monkeys live in the jungle. Ask the children to imagine what other animals might live there. Show them some information books that have pictures of different jungle environments and talk about these together.

Provide each child with a piece of paper and some colouring and drawing materials. Ask them to draw a picture of the thick jungle where Rama and Sita

lived. Encourage them to use a combination of their creativity and the pictures that they have seen in the information books. Suggest that they include elements from the story such as the beautiful plants and flowers, and Ravana, the king of the demons, who had ten heads and ten arms.

Support
Help the children to draw very simple jungle pictures based on their imaginations but also on their knowledge of well-known stories such as *Elmer* by David McKee (Red Fox) and *Where the Wild Things Are* by Maurice Sendak (Red Fox).

Extension
Help the children to use and develop the technical vocabulary needed to describe their pictures as they work, including features such as rivers, lakes, bridges, vines, rainforest trees, specific animals and so on. Encourage them to add as much detail as possible to their pictures. Suggest that they add collage materials to enhance their pictures.

Home links
Explain to parents and carers that you are learning about the festival of Divali. Let the children take their jungle pictures home together with a copy of the story on the photocopiable sheet on page 75. Encourage parents and carers to share the story with their children and to help them to describe their jungle picture.

Going fishing

What you need
A computer with a painting program; acetate sheets (such as those used on an overhead projector); pen (suitable for using on acetates); sticky tape; picture or drawing of the Scottish flag; information books about fishing and the sea; paper; colouring materials.

Preparation
Draw some simple shapes of fishing boats and equipment onto acetate sheets.

What to do
Tell the children that St Andrew, who is the patron saint of Scotland, was one of Jesus' disciples and a fisherman. St Andrew was crucified on a diagonal cross and buried in Scotland. This cross, which is called the St Andrew's Cross, forms part of the Scottish flag, appearing against a blue background which signifies his connection to the sea.

Look at some information books about fishing and the sea with the children. Pay particular attention to the fishing boats and other fishing equipment such as nets, buoys and floats.

Now show the children your acetate drawings of fishing boats and equipment and explain that you will be fixing these to the computer screen for the children to use to trace the outlines with a painting program.

Once all the children have had a turn at making their fishing pictures on the computer, show them a picture of the

Scottish flag, explaining its links to St Andrew. Ask them to think about what they would like to put on a flag for St Andrew. Encourage them to imagine his life as a fisherman and discuss his connections to the sea. Give each child a piece of paper and some colouring materials and ask them to draw a new flag for St Andrew using the ideas that you have talked about together.

Support
Make very simple acetate templates and work closely with the children to help them develop their mouse control skills. Alternatively, use a Clip Art program or a concept keyboard to create very simple boats and sea-related pictures.

Extension
Let the children attempt copying and printing out their flag designs by using the painting program on the computer.

Free kitchen

What you need
The photocopiable sheet on page 76; ingredients for making chapattis and raita (see the photocopiable sheet); aprons; two mixing bowls; heavy frying pan; fish slice; rolling-pin; teaspoon; sharp knife; serving bowls and plates; hob; refrigerator.

What to do
Explain to the children that this Sikh festival celebrates the birthday of Guru Nanak who was the founder of the Sikh faith. Guru Nanak started the Sikh faith from his belief that all people should work together and worship one god. He introduced the idea of the 'langar' (free kitchen) to help the needy and the poor. Together, talk about ways that people can help the poor and needy today.

Ask the children to wash their hands and put on the aprons. Use the recipes on the photocopiable sheet to make some traditional vegetarian food, chapattis and raita, with the children. Once the chapattis have cooled, cut them into small strips and ask the children to arrange them on serving plates. Put the chilled raita into serving bowls. Let the children taste the food that they have made. Remind them of Guru Nanak's free kitchen and of the traditional Sikh custom of hospitality.

Tell the children that you are going to invite some other people to come and share the food that you have all prepared together. If your group is attached to a school, host your free kitchen at playtime and invite the other children to come and join you. Otherwise, invite parents and carers to come fifteen minutes before the end of the session to try the chapattis and raita. Encourage the children in the group to serve them.

Support
Talk about birthdays in general with the children. Ask them about the sorts of things they eat at birthday parties. Do they help to make any of them?

Extension
Make other traditional vegetarian foods such as samosas and dhal. Hold a feast and encourage the children to remember the Sikh custom of hospitality by serving each other the dishes that they helped to make.

Model temple

What you need
Access to or knowledge of the story of Hanukkah, such as in *Autumn and Winter Festivals* by Carole Court (*Themes for Early Years* series, Scholastic); pictures and photographs of Jewish temples and synagogues; a picture of the temple in Jerusalem (if possible); a selection of junk materials; paints; collage materials; glue; sticky tape; scissors; card; paper.

Preparation
Find a selection of pictures of Jewish temples and synagogues to show to the children. If possible, pay a visit to a temple in your area before beginning this activity.

What to do
Tell the children the story of Hanukkah, focusing on how the soldiers stole the objects from the temple and spoiled the sacred and peaceful nature of it. Help the children to appreciate the importance and significance of the temple to the Jewish people.

Show the children the pictures of synagogues and temples that you have collected and discuss them together. What shapes, patterns and colours can the children see in the pictures? Encourage them to describe the way that the temples are built and decorated.

Now provide the children with a selection of junk materials and explain that you would like them to try to make a model temple. Invite them to examine the shapes of the objects and look again at the pictures. Are any of the materials suitable? Encourage the children to choose the boxes and tubes that they need to construct their temple. Suggest that they place them next to each other first before they stick them together and decorate them. Once the children are happy with the shape of their temples, let them choose from the paints and collage materials to decorate them. Remind the children to look at the pictures of the temples to give them an idea of how temples are decorated.

Support
Select the relevant junk materials for the children and help them to decorate and fix them together.

Extension
Invite the children to draw a plan of their temple on paper before they begin to design and make it.

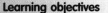

Winter soup

What you need
Selection of winter vegetables; large saucepan; wooden spoon; hob; measuring jug; scales; sieve; sharp knife; ladle; serving bowls; spoons; aprons; 30g butter; 500g leeks; an onion; 900ml vegetable stock; 350g potatoes; 300ml milk; salt; pepper.

Preparation
Trim and slice the leeks. Peel the potatoes and cut them into chunks. Chop the onion. Ask the children to wash their hands and put on aprons.

What to do
Show the children your selection of winter vegetables and invite them to handle and describe them. Do they know what they are and what they taste like? Which vegetables do the children like best?

Explain to the children that one of the ways to keep warm in winter is to eat hot nutritious foods such as soups to give our bodies the energy needed to keep warm. Tell the children that they are going to help you to make a winter potato and leek soup to warm everyone up!

Melt the butter in a large saucepan and invite the children to describe what has happened to it. Add the leeks and onion and cook for about ten minutes until softened. Encourage the children to take it in turns to stir the vegetables and to describe the way they change as they are cooking. Add

the stock and the potato chunks, bring to the boil and then cover and simmer for about 30 minutes.

Once the vegetables have cooled slightly, let the children help you to rub the soup through a sieve, using the back of a wooden spoon. What has happened to the potatoes? Have any of the children ever helped to mash potatoes before?

Return all the vegetables to the pan and add the milk, salt and pepper. Allow the children to stir occasionally. When the soup is piping hot, serve it into several small bowls and allow the children to taste it when it has cooled to a suitable temperature.

Support
Simplify the activity by making mashed potatoes, discussing with the children the changes between raw and cooked potatoes.

Extension
Involve the children in the weighing and preparation of the vegetables.

Learning objectives
To find out about and identify some features of events they observe; to look closely at change.

Group size
Small groups.

Home links
Encourage parents and carers to spend some time cooking with their children. Suggest that they discuss the changes to the foods when they are cooked.

All about ice

Learning objectives
To look closely at change; to find out about some features of events they observe.

Group size
Small groups.

What you need
A story about ice and snow such as *Little Mo* by Martin Waddell (Walker Books); water; ice-cube trays; a frozen food compartment of a fridge; plates.

Preparation
Read the story to the children. Talk about the ice and snow in the story. Have the children ever seen ice, snow or frost? What do they look and feel like? Ice, snow and frost do not last forever, so what happens to them and why? Talk about melting with the children and explain that ice, frost and snow only last when it is very cold, and as soon as it gets warm they melt and turn to water.

Now explain that you are going to make ice cubes together. Fill an ice-cube tray with water and ask the children for ideas of places to put it to turn it to ice. Remind them that the place needs to be very, very cold. What places do the children consider as being very cold? Put the ice tray in a frozen food compartment of a fridge and explain that you will check it later (or the next day) to see if the water has turned to ice.

What to do
When the ice cubes are ready, look at them with the children. Let each child touch the surface of the cubes and encourage them to describe how they feel. Ask the children for ideas of how to turn the ice cubes back to water again. Give each child an ice cube and ask them to put it on a plate somewhere where they think it will melt quickly. Can they guess which of the chosen spots will make the cube melt the most quickly? Encourage them to give reasons for their answers.

Support
Keep the activity simple for the children by demonstrating how to make ice and then melting it again. Relate to the children's experiences such as eating a dripping ice lolly as it melts in the sunshine.

Extension
Carry out a more structured investigation with the children by asking them to put their ice cubes in three distinct places and to help you make a chart of predictions, observations and conclusions.

Winter birds

What you need
The photocopiable sheet on page 77; coloured pencils; colour illustrated bird guide; bird feeders; bird-table (optional); bird bath (or dish of water, raised above the ground); bird food.

Preparation
Make an enlarged copy of the photocopiable sheet.

What to do
Talk to the children about the birds that they might see during the winter. Show them the enlarged copy of the photocopiable sheet and tell them the name of each of the birds. Do they recognize some of the birds? What colours are they?

Explain to the children that birds find it hard to get enough food in the winter because the ground is often frozen and hard, and the water freezes over, making it difficult to get a drink. There are also fewer insects and fruit around in the winter.

Ask the children how they might help the birds during the winter? Ideas might include hanging up bird feeders, putting out a bird-table, bird bath or dish of water (away from places where cats might reach the birds). Decide on the action that your group would like to take and set up a bird-feeding station, within view of a window.

After a few weeks, if kept well stocked, the children will begin to see birds at your feeding station on a regular basis. Make copies of the photocopiable sheet and place them near the window.

Once the children are familiar with some of the birds, provide them with their own copy of the photocopiable sheet and some coloured pencils. Work with small groups of children at a time and ask them to colour the birds the appropriate colours, using a bird guidebook to check the colours if necessary.

Support
Focus on three of the most easily identified birds such as the robin, blackbird and blue tit.

Extension
Encourage the children to use their bird guide photocopiable sheets as the first page of a nature diary. Ask them to draw other identification guides, such as leaves, trees and insects, to include in their diaries and share with the rest of the group.

Light and heat

What you need
A large piece of paper or a board; pictures from magazines or catalogues and objects that give you light or warmth such as candle, lamps, torch, scarf, gloves, radiator and so on; sugar paper; glue; scissors; pencils.

Preparation
Cut out 'light' and 'heat' pictures.

What to do
Talk with the children about winter weather and how it is often very cold. In winter we also have much more darkness than in the summer months. If your group operates long hours, the children will be aware that in the winter it is often dark when they go home. Remind the children how in the summer-time they can play outside until much later than they do during the winter.

Ask the children to brainstorm a list of ideas for keeping warm in the winter, such as wearing winter coats or sitting by the fire. Write their ideas onto a large piece of paper or on a board. Then repeat the process, this time asking the children to think of a list of ideas for ways to make light when it is dark outside.

Present the children with a wide variety of objects and pictures. Discuss what the objects are and what the pictures show and ask the children to sort them into two sets – 'Things that keep you warm' and 'Things that give light'. Are there any that give light and keep you warm?

Now provide the children with some sugar paper and an assortment of 'light' and 'heat' pictures. Ask them to choose either 'light' or 'heat' pictures to make a collage poster about getting warmth or light in the winter. Share the children's posters at circle time.

Support
Let the children choose from a limited selection of objects and pictures.

Extension
Encourage the children to sort the objects and pictures in more sophisticated ways, such as which objects use electricity, or which objects can be worn.

Pop-up snowman

What you need
The photocopiable sheet on page 78; scissors; two pieces of A4 blue paper per child; glue sticks; ruler; white or silver pencils or pens; pencils; colouring materials.

Preparation
Make a copy of the photocopiable sheet for each child. Follow the instructions below to prepare one of the pop-up cards to show to the children.

What to do
Explain to the children that you are going to help them to make a special pop-up snowman card. Show them the one you have already made and let the children look carefully at it.

Give each child two pieces of blue paper and ask them to fold one of the pieces in half so that the short edges meet. Help them to draw lines of about 3cm in length, 9cm from each end of the folded edge (see 1 on the photocopiable sheet). Cut along both lines and fold over the flap both ways to crease it. Unfold the flap, open the card and pinch along the middle fold (on either side of the flap) to crease it the other way. Now push the flap down with your finger and close the card. Open the card and the flap should pop up in a box shape. Fold the other piece of paper and glue it to the first piece (see 2 on the photocopiable sheet).

Now give each child a copy of the photocopiable sheet and ask them to cut out and decorate the snowman. Show them how to carefully glue their finished snowman onto the front of the pop-up box (see right). Encourage the children to complete their artwork by drawing snowflakes in the background with white or silver pencils.

Support
Make the box-fold section of the pop-up card for the children and invite them to focus on cutting out and decorating their snowman and gluing it into place.

Extension
Challenge the children to add extra details to the background of their cards, such as snow-covered trees and bushes or a glowing moon.

Winter clothes game

Learning objective
To find out about the winter weather and how it affects what we wear.

Group size
Two to four children.

What you need
The photocopiable sheet on page 79; colouring materials; a dice with 1–3 dots; counters or playing pieces; sets of winter clothes for dressing-up.

Preparation
Make a copy of the photocopiable sheet for each child.

What to do
Show the children the winter dressing-up clothes and talk about the sort of clothes that people need to wear in the cold weather. Ask the children to talk about the clothes that they like to wear to keep them warm.

Work with two to four children at a time and give each child a copy of the photocopiable sheet, a counter and some colouring materials. Explain that

you are going to play a game together that involves going from home to the group, collecting winter clothes along the way. Explain to the children how to play the game:
◆ The object of the game is for a player to collect all five pieces of clothing (by landing on the different pictures and colouring in the matching pictures at the bottom of the sheet) before getting to the finish or 'setting' square. A player can only finish by landing on the group square having collected (and coloured in) all the five types of clothing.
◆ A player throws the dice and can then move in any direction. It is obviously best to try to land on a piece of clothing that has not already been collected! (This will involve the children in employing tactics and logical thought.)

Play the 'Winter clothes game' with the children, encouraging them to make decisions as to which direction to move their counter.

Support
Some children may need support to count the dots on the dice using one-to-one correspondence. Help them to point to each dot as they count and to point to each square as they move their playing pieces.

Extension
Vary the game by using a normal dice (1–6 dots) and playing a 'beetle' style version, where each item of clothing is assigned a number from 1 to 5, such as '1' for a scarf, '2' for a hat, '3' for a coat, '4' for a pair of mittens and '5' for a pair of boots. The children have to throw a '6' to draw a body and then take turns to throw the dice and add the items of clothing until they have all five items. The winner is the first child to have a fully-clothed body shape.

Home links
Let the children take home a copy of the game to play with their parents or carers.

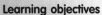
Sunrise and sunset

What you need
A piece of A3 plain paper per child; white and yellow card; scissors; glue; pencils; colouring materials.

Preparation
Make a zigzag book for each child by folding the A3 paper into thirds. Write the words 'At sunset…' on the first page, 'When the moon comes up…' on the second page and 'At sunrise…' on the third page. Cut out a crescent moon shape from the white card and two semicircle suns from the yellow card for each child (the shapes should fit onto the pages of the zigzag books, see right).

What to do
Talk to the children about night and day. What happens at the different times? Explain that night-time falls when the sun sets, and that daytime begins again when the sun rises. Tell the children about the Muslim period of Ramadan. Explain that during this time, the Muslim people fast between sunrise and sunset. Many Muslim people get up early to eat their breakfast before sunrise and don't eat again until after the sun has set.

Work with small groups of children and give each child a zigzag book, two card suns and a moon. Read the words in the books together and help each child to glue their suns and moon in the correct places. Talk together about the things that happen at sunset,

during the night (when the moon comes up) and at sunrise. Encourage the children to think about what they do at those times and also talk about what some animals do, such as 'When the moon comes up, the owls wake up and look for food'. Scribe the children's ideas onto their books for them and ask them to add pictures to illustrate them.

Support
Make up simple sentences in the zigzag books for the children, for example, 'At the end of the day…', 'During the night…' and 'At the beginning of the day…'.

Extension
Encourage the children to fold their own books and cut out their own moon and sun shapes.

Computer calendars

What you need
A computer with a word-processing
program; red or green sugar paper
(A3 size); scissors; paper; glue sticks;
sticky tape; magazines; catalogues; old
Christmas cards; colouring materials;
ribbon.

What to do
Explain to the children that Advent is a
period of four weeks leading up to the
festival of Christmas. Tell the children
that an Advent calendar is a special

big enough, but not too big, so that
they all fit onto an A3 sheet of sugar
paper. The children will be using them
as flaps under which they will draw or
stick Christmas pictures.

Let each child have a turn at using
the computer to design their own set of
numbers. Help them to cut out their
numbers (in squares in order to use the
numbers as flaps) and ask them to stick
their numbers randomly onto their piece
of sugar paper. They must only stick the
top part of the number to the paper, so
that the number squares
can be lifted as flaps.

Now ask the children to
cut out pictures from old
Christmas cards, catalogues
and magazines, or to draw
their own Christmas
images on paper to cut
out and stick in place.
Ensure that the pictures
are the same size as their
number squares and stick
the pictures underneath
each number. Encourage
the children to use a
mixture of techniques to
carry out this sticking
activity.

Once the children have
added all their pictures,
help them to attach
ribbon hooks to the top of
their calendars.

calendar that is used from 1 to 24
December. Tell the children that you are
going to help them to make their own
Advent calendars.

Start by helping one of the children
to key in the numbers from 1 to 24 on
the computer. Leave plenty of space
between each number as the children
will be cutting the numbers out. Show
them how to experiment with colour,
size and font to achieve the desired
effect. Make sure that the numbers are

Support
Cut out the numbers and a selection of
Christmas images ready for the children
to use.

Extension
If you have some Christmas Clip Art,
encourage the children to experiment
with it to make repeating patterns and
use them as borders to decorate their
Advent calendars.

Looking after Santa

What you need
A large piece of paper or a board; junk materials including boxes of different sizes; scissors; glue; sticky tape; collage materials including fabric scraps; paints; colouring materials; Plasticine; construction toys such as Lego.

Preparation
Gather together a range of junk and collage materials suitable for making a sleigh and equipment for Santa.

What to do
Ask the children to tell you what they know about Santa Claus. What does he have to do every Christmas Eve? Do the children think he has to make a long journey? What long journeys have they made? What things do they need when they go on a long journey?

Encourage the children to think about Santa's needs – such as food and warmth, a sturdy sack, warm mittens and a good strong sleigh. Write the children's ideas onto a large piece of paper or a board.

In small groups, ask the children to use the junk or construction materials to make a strong sleigh for Santa. Encourage them to leave enough room inside the sleigh for Santa to sit and for them to be able to pack it with items that Santa and his reindeers will need for their long journey. Work closely with the groups and help them to select suitable materials.

Demonstrate different ways of fixing the materials together and encourage the children to choose the appropriate one. Once they have completed their sleighs, remind them of the list of things that Santa and his reindeers will need. Let the children choose some of these things and suggest that they use the collage, construction materials and Plasticine to make them. For example, they might want to make some carrots

from Plasticine or a blanket from material scraps.

Support
Provide the children with boxes cut into the shape of a sleigh. Ask them to decorate them and encourage them to fill the sleigh with three or four things that Santa will need on his journey.

Extension
Challenge the children to make a greater selection of goodies for Santa and his reindeers. Encourage them to show their models to the rest of the group at circle time, explaining how each object should be used.

All about Eid

What you need
Small dolls or puppets; dolls' clothes; Plasticine or salt dough; collage, construction and junk materials; card; paper; scissors; glue; colouring materials.

Preparation
Set up the range of different materials on separate tables. Familiarize yourself with the festival of Eid-ul-Fitr which is a fast-breaking festival and falls after the month of Ramadan when Muslim people fast for a month. The religion of Islam uses the phases of the moon to measure its months. On the last night of Ramadan, when a new moon is expected, many people crowd the streets looking for the sign that Ramadan is over. People visit the mosque at dawn to say special prayers and to give money to charity.

What to do
Describe the festival of Eid-ul-Fitr to the children, drawing out the important factors of the celebrations such as breaking the fast, praying at the mosque, giving money to the poor, making up after quarrels, wearing new clothes and giving presents.

Ask the children to work in small groups or pairs and suggest that they use dolls or puppets to act out the main features of the festival. Suggest that they start by dressing their dolls or puppets in special clothes. Remind them of the traditional activities that the Muslim people take part in during the festival, such as going to the mosque and giving presents and cards to each other. Show the children the different materials set out on the tables and encourage them to use them for their Eid celebrations. Explain that the Plasticine or salt dough can be used to make pretend food for a feast, the card and paper can be used for making Eid cards and the collage, junk and construction materials can be used for making presents to give to each other.

Support
Concentrate on one or two aspects of the festival, such as dressing the dolls in special clothes and making some Plasticine food for a feast.

Extension
Make a display of the pretend food, gifts and cards that the children have made for their Eid celebrations.

Millennium Eve

What you need
Pictures, souvenirs and memorabilia of the millennium celebrations such as newspaper cuttings, T-shirts, souvenir publications, coins and so on; display table.

Preparation
Find out how the millennium was celebrated in your local area. Take photographs of any monuments or public facilities that were erected to commemorate the event. Make a collection of any millennium memorabilia.

What to do
Remaining sensitive to individual circumstances, find out if the children have any personal memories of 31 December 1999 – Millennium Eve. Ask them if they can remember going to a big party or to see fireworks. Did some of them watch on television the events taking place around the world? Explain that the Millennium Eve celebrations

were the biggest New Year celebrations of the Christian calendar ever seen.

Encourage the children to take turns to talk about their memories of the occasion. Show them some of the memorabilia that you have collected. Explain that around the United Kingdom, there were special events and parties to mark the occasion. Most towns and cities organized tree-planting activities and erected special monuments and public facilities such as art galleries, parks, monuments and new sports centres for the year 2000. Show the children your photographs of the local places of interest and encourage them to tell you about any visits that they have made to them.

On a national scale, did the children pay a visit to places such as the Millennium Dome in London or to the BBC's Futureworld exhibitions?

Support
If the children cannot remember Millennium Eve, ask them to think about any other New Year celebrations or big celebrations that they have been to. Invite them to share their memories with the rest of the group.

Extension
With the children's help, set up a display of millennium memories and memorabilia in your own setting. Invite older children to contribute their memories through shared writing and illustrations.

Learning objective
To observe, find out
about and identify
features in the place
they live and the
natural world.

Group size
Whole group for
discussion; small
groups for activity.

Sand maps

What you need
The photocopiable sheet on page 80;
sand tray; small rocks; pebbles; blue
Cellophane; small-world toys; toy
animals; twigs; pieces of foliage.

What to do
Read the story 'Chinese New Year' on
the photocopiable sheet to the
children. Discuss the different animals
together. Which ones are generally fast
and which ones are generally slow?
Which ones did they expect to come
first and last?

Now work with small groups of
children and explain that you would
like them to set up an obstacle course
for some toy animals in the sand tray.
Ask the children for ideas of features to
include such as a lake or river, river
banks, rocks and trees. Help the
children to learn and use the relevant
geographical vocabulary.
Provide them with small rocks, pebbles,
some water to make wet sand,
Cellophane pieces for a river or lake,
small-world toys such as trees and
bushes, natural materials such as twigs
and pieces of foliage. Let the children

work as a group to put the objects into
place in the sand tray.

Once the obstacle course has been
set up, ask the children to take turns to
place the animals in the sand tray,
according to your directions such as
'Put the lion next to the big tree' or
'Put the giraffe in front of the rocks'
and so on. Vary the game by letting
each child place an animal in the sand
tray. Describe the position of each
animal (without saying its name) and
ask the children to tell you which
animal you are referring to.

Finish by allowing the children, in
pairs, to play freely with the animals in
the sand tray.

Support
Work with only two or three children at
a time and give each child just one
specific job to do as the pair or group
sets up the obstacle course.

Extension
Suggest that the children work with a
partner and use the sand tray to make
up their own version of the animals'
race story together.

Home links
Let each child take
home a copy of the
story to share and
enjoy with their
parents or carers.

All about weddings

Learning objectives
To find out about past and present events in their own lives; to learn about the cultures and beliefs of other people.

Group size
Whole group.

What you need
A collection of traditional and contemporary stories with love and weddings as a central theme such as 'Cinderella' and 'Beauty and the Beast'.

Preparation
Find out about a range of cultural wedding traditions. A good source of information can be found by accessing the 'Yahoo!' Internet site (www.yahoo.com) and doing a search on religion and religious practices and ceremonies.

What to do
Tell the children that St Valentine is the special saint of people in love. Ask the children to think of any stories about love and weddings that they have heard. Remind them of some well-known traditional tales such as 'Cinderella' and 'Beauty and the Beast'. Tell them their favourite tale from the ones that they have remembered.

Now ask the children if they have ever been to any weddings. Ask them to tell one another about their experiences. Can they remember anything about the traditions at the wedding that they went to, such as cutting the cake, giving presents, throwing confetti, wearing flowers and so on?

If possible, find out about a range of different cultural wedding traditions to talk to the children about. For example, in Hindu weddings, the couple exchange garlands in order to welcome each other into their lives. They also exchange gold rings. This represents a long married life as gold lasts forever. They believe that the fourth finger of the hand has a vein leading directly to the heart – the groom wears the ring on the fourth finger of his right hand and the bride wears hers on the fourth finger of her left hand so as to form a complete heart.

Support
Concentrate on the theme of love and marriage found in the children's favourite traditional tales.

Extension
Assist the children in making envelopes of confetti by cutting out heart and petal shapes from tissue paper. Make flower garlands from scrunched-up tissue paper stapled to strips of green crêpe paper.

Home links
Invite the children to bring in any photographs of family weddings or weddings that they have been to. Encourage them to talk about and share these photos at circle time.

Animal parade

What you need
Illustrated animal information books;
simple mask templates; string or
ribbon; stapler; glue; paints; collage
and colouring materials; music such as
the soundtracks from the Disney movies
The Lion King or *Jungle Book* (Disney).

What to do
Explain to the children that before the
beginning of the Christian season of
Lent, some countries hold colourful and
noisy Mardi Gras parades or carnivals.

animals? Do they like their colours? Do
they like their behaviour? Do they like
their patterned fur? Encourage each
child to choose an animal in turn and
to read and talk about it.

Now provide each child with a
simple mask template and a selection
of paints, collage and colouring
materials. Encourage them tell you how
they would like to decorate their mask
to look like their chosen animal and
then help them to plan it. Remind
them of the colours of their animal and
the texture of its skin or
fur. Provide help where
necessary as the children
decorate their mask. Invite
them to attach string or
ribbon to fasten their
masks and assist them in
doing so.

When each group of
children has finished their
masks, work all together to
sort the animals into sets
such as birds, fish, African
animals and so on. Hold
an 'animal parade' and
encourage the children to
march in their different
animal sets to music such
as the soundtrack from
The Lion King or *Jungle
Book*.

During these parades, people dress up
in fantastic costumes and wear
elaborate masks and head-dresses.

Tell the children that they are all
going to take part in a small Mardi Gras
carnival of their own and that you
would like them to make special animal
masks to wear in the parade.

Put the children into small groups
and, together, look at some illustrated
information books about animals,
discussing the children's favourite ones.
What do they like about their chosen

Support
Let the children choose from a selection
of only three animals and provide them
with more structured help to decorate
their masks.

Extension
Invite the children to share their
animal masks at circle time and
encourage them to remember at least
two facts about their chosen animals.
Ask the children to tell these to the rest
of the group.

The ugly duckling

One spring time, five eggs lay in a nest. It was near the water, on an island in the middle of a lake. Two big, white water birds looked after the eggs. The mother bird sat on them to keep them warm. They both guarded the nest to keep it safe. Soon the eggs hatched. The parent birds were very pleased to see their fluffy brown babies. They brought insects and waterweeds for them to eat, and bread that people threw into the water for them.

The parent birds took the babies for rides on their backs. Soon they learned how to swim, following their father and mother. One day, a cruel boy came to the lake. He threw stones at them and frightened them. The father bird flew at the boy, and knocked him down, and the mother bird flew back to the island in the middle of the lake. The babies didn't know where to go. They paddled away as fast as they could, and found places to hide.

One little bird scrambled to the water's edge, and ran away. He hid in the tall reeds beside another lake. Some shiny blue and green ducks swam by. 'Go away,' they said crossly. 'This is our lake, and we don't want ugly ducklings like you here.' The baby bird felt sad and lonely. He had lost all his family, and no one liked him. The water was like a mirror. He looked at his reflection. 'It's true! I'm really ugly,' he thought. He hid his head under his wing, and tried to go to sleep.

All through the hot summer and the cold winter, he hid in the reeds. At last, the spring came, and some beautiful white birds came swimming across the lake. When they saw him, they said, 'Come with us, brother.' He was astonished. 'You don't want an ugly duckling like me with you,' he said. 'Ugly? Have you looked at yourself lately?' one asked. The little bird looked at his reflection in the water. His dull brown feathers had gone, and his new feathers were white as snow! 'You're a swan, like us,' said the birds. The little bird was overjoyed. He swam out of the reeds, and sailed across the lake holding his head high, with the beautiful swans.

Barbara Moore

The story of Holi

Hiranyakashup was a powerful king. He was so proud that he thought he was God. Prahlad was his little boy. Everyone told Prahlad that Hiranyakashup was God, so he thought this was true.

When Prahlad grew up, he met a man who made pots. The potter was praying to God. He was very upset. Prahlad asked, 'What's the matter? Are you praying to king Hiranyakashup?' The potter said, 'No, Hiranyakashup is a king, but kings are only men. I'm praying to Lord Vishnu* to save some kittens. A mother cat put them into a pot I'd just made. I didn't know they were there. Now I've put the pots into the hot oven to bake hard, and I'm afraid the kittens will die.' When the potter opened the oven door, Prahlad heard a little sound – 'Miaow! Miaow!' The kittens were alive! God had saved them.

Now Prahlad knew Hiranyakashup was not God. He prayed to Vishnu instead. The king was angry. He began to hate Prahlad, and tried to get rid of him. His soldiers dug a deep pit and filled it with poisonous snakes. Big snakes, little snakes, long snakes and short snakes, patterned snakes and plain snakes twisted and hissed at the bottom of the pit.

The soldiers threw Prahlad in. The snakes wriggled and slithered all over Prahlad, but they didn't bite him, because God was watching, and saved him.

Hiranyakashup was even angrier. When Prahlad was sleeping on the ground, he sent elephants to trample over him, but they walked carefully all around Prahlad, and God saved him. Next, the wicked king sent soldiers to kill Prahlad with their swords, but God was watching, and saved him again.

The king was furious. He asked Holika, his sister, for help. Holika had magic powers – fire couldn't burn her. Hiranyakashup's soldiers built a huge bonfire, and Holika tricked Prahlad into climbing up to the top with her. The soldiers lit the bonfire. But God was watching and saved Prahlad from the flames. He broke Holika's magic spell, so that she was the one who was burnt in the fire.

At Holi, Hindus remember this story, and light bonfires to remind them about it.

*Vishnu is a name Hindu people give to God

Barbara Moore

The story of Baisakhi

Guru Nanak was a good and holy man who started the Sikh religion. He taught people that they should be friends, even if they prayed to God in different ways. But Guru Nanak had died long ago. Now the Sikhs were being attacked by people who hated them. Men, women and children were being killed. Guru Gobind Singh was the Sikhs' new teacher and leader. He was very worried. Guru Nanak had taught that everyone should live in peace with their neighbours, but the Sikhs' neighbours wouldn't let them live in peace. What should they do?

Thousands of people met to hear what Guru Gobind Singh would say. The crowd went quiet as their leader came out of his tent. He was wearing a yellow tunic, with a blue sash around the middle. On his head he wore a turban, and he carried a sword in his hand. 'Who is ready to give up his life for God?' he shouted. Nobody spoke. At last, one man stepped forward. 'I am not afraid to die,' he said. The Guru led him into the tent. There was a thud, and the Guru came out by himself, with blood dripping from his sword. The crowd was shocked and silent.

They thought that the Guru had chopped off the head of the brave man. Again, the Guru shouted, 'Will anyone else give me his head?' After a while, another brave man stepped forward. The Guru led him into his tent, and again there was a thud. The Guru came out alone. Three more times he asked the same question, and three more men went into the tent.

Then the Guru came out again. Everyone gasped in astonishment. He was not alone – all the men who had gone into the tent came out with him! They weren't dead, after all. They were wearing yellow tunics and blue sashes and turbans, like the Guru. The Guru spoke to the crowd. 'These five brave men were ready to die for God. From now on, they are the Five Beloved – they are soldiers of God, and the new brotherhood of the Sikhs. We will fight to protect the poor and weak and helpless.'

Now Sikhs all over the world remember this story, and celebrate every year with the festival of Baisakhi.

Barbara Moore

Days gone by

Talk about the picture.

EARLY YEARS AROUND THE YEAR Knowledge and understanding of the world

Keeping cool

Talk about these pictures.

Lights and lanterns

Talk about the different kinds of lights.

EARLY YEARS AROUND THE YEAR Knowledge and understanding of the world

Keeping dry

Rain on the green grass,
And rain on the tree,
Rain on the house-top,
But not on me.

Rain, rain go away,
Come again another day.

It's raining, it's pouring,
The old man is snoring;
He went to bed
And bumped his head
And couldn't get up in the morning.

All traditional

Autumn is here

In country village,
In city and town,
Shades of green
Are turning brown.

The sun grows weak,
The sky looks grey;
And night grows longer
Than the day.

While, out-of-doors,
For young and old,
Coats keep out
The rain and cold.

In many shops
The lights are on –
The summer sun
Has long since gone.

It's autumn and
The time of year
Acorns are gathered
And berries appear.

While leaves on trees,
In lane and town,
Turn rustic red
And golden brown.

Some leaves will fall
And cloak the street.
(Just hear them SCRUNCH
Beneath your feet!)

Soon birds will fly
To a warmer clime –
For after autumn
Comes wintertime.

But now, in autumn,
All's green and brown,
In country village –
In city – and town!

Trevor Harvey

Leaf models

Cut out the leaf templates.

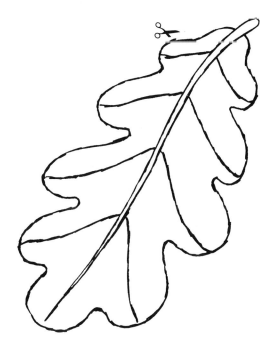

Shelters

Talk about the different shelters.

The story of Divali

Prince Rama's father was the king. He wanted Rama to be the new king when he died, but because of a promise he had made, he had to send Rama and his wife Sita away for fourteen years. Rama's brother Lakshman went too.

One day, Rama's brother Bharat came to tell him that the old king had died. 'Come home, Rama,' he said, but Rama replied. 'I promised to stay away for fourteen years.' Bharat said, 'I will look after everything for you, but I will put your golden slippers on the King's throne to show that you are the real king, not me.'

Rama, Sita and Lakshman lived happily in the jungle. They built a hut and grew things to eat. Beautiful plants and flowers and fruit grew in the thick, shady forest, and hundreds of animals and birds lived there. But in the deepest and darkest parts of the jungle lived demons with magic powers. Ravana was the king of the demons. He had ten heads and ten arms. When he saw Sita, he wanted her for his wife. He sent a golden deer. Sita wanted Rama to keep it for a pet, so Rama ran after it, calling to Lakshman, 'Take care of Sita! This may be a magic trick!' Deep in the jungle, the deer called out in Rama's voice, 'Lakshman, help! Help!' Lakshman thought Rama was in trouble. He drew a magic circle around Sita, and cried, 'You will be safe in here!'

Then he ran off to help Rama.

Sita was all alone. Ravana took the shape of a poor old man. He pretended to be tired and ill. Sita went to help him. She stepped outside the magic circle, and Ravana changed back to his own dreadful shape. No one heard Sita calling for help. Ravana carried her away across the sea in his flying chariot, and locked her in his castle on the island of Lanka.

When Rama and Lakshman came back, Sita was gone. They looked for her for years. At last, they met Hanuman, the king of the monkeys, who told them that Ravana had got her. With an army of monkeys, they set off to rescue her. After a terrible fight with the demons, Rama killed Ravana with a magic arrow.

Now fourteen years had gone by, and it was time to go home. Rama's brother Bharat was waiting to meet them, and everyone came out into the dark streets with little lamps. (The lamps were called divas, and that is how Divali, the Festival of Light, got its name.) Every year, at Divali time, people remember how the wicked demon Ravana was killed, and they light candles to remind them of when Rama and Sita came home to be king and queen.

Barbara Moore

Free kitchen

Recipe card

Chapattis
250g wholemeal flour
1 tsp salt
200ml water
cooking oil

What to do
◆ Mix the flour and salt in a bowl and make a well in the centre.
◆ Pour in the water gradually and mix until you have a soft dough.
◆ Knead the dough for five minutes and leave to prove for half an hour.
◆ Divide into egg-size portions and knead again.
◆ Roll out into 10cm circles.
◆ Cook the chapattis in the oil on a low heat until they blister (adults only). Press them down with a fish slice.

Raita
300ml natural yoghurt
½ cucumber
2 tbsp chopped mint
pinch of salt and black pepper

What to do
◆ Peel the cucumber and slice lengthways from top to bottom.
◆ Cut the slices into 3cm long pieces.
◆ Mix the cucumber into the yoghurt with the other ingredients.
◆ Cover and chill for about half an hour.

Winter birds

Try to spot these birds outside.

sparrow

blue tit

blackbird

robin

thrush

Pop-up snowman

Cut out the snowman and make a pop-up card.

EARLY YEARS AROUND THE YEAR Knowledge and understanding of the world

Winter clothes game

Chinese New Year

It was nearly New Year, and twelve animals were quarrelling. Each one wanted the New Year to be called after him. 'I'm the biggest, so it should be the Year of the Dragon!' roared Dragon. Little Rat squeaked. 'But I'm the cleverest, so it should be called the Year of the Rat!'

'Oh, no you're not!' all the others shouted. The Gods came to see what was the matter.

'What are you quarrelling about?' they asked. They all started to answer together. What a noise! Pig grunted, Dog barked, Rat squeaked, Dragon roared, Ox lowed, Tiger growled, Hare squealed, Snake hissed, Horse neighed, Ram bleated, Cockerel crowed, and Monkey chattered. 'Be quiet!' ordered the Gods. 'We have thought of a way to settle this quarrel.' There was a river nearby. It was wide and deep. 'You must have a race across the river. We will call the New Year after the winner of the race.'

The animals lined up on the bank of the river. Each one thought he would be the winner. 'Ready, steady, go!' With a mighty splash, they all jumped into the water, and started to swim as fast as they could. Ox

was a good swimmer. Soon, he was in front. Little Rat was a good swimmer, too, but not as fast as Ox. Ox's tail was just in front of his nose. He grabbed it, and climbed onto Ox's back. Just as Ox was about to win, Rat jumped over his head, and landed in front of him. 'Hooray! I'm the winner!' he squeaked. Ox was astonished. 'Where did you come from?' he asked, but Rat just laughed. The Gods laughed, too, and said, 'Rat, you came first, so the New Year will be called the Year of the Rat. Ox, you were second, so next year will be the Year of the Ox.'

One by one, the other animals finished the race. Tiger came third, Hare fourth, Dragon fifth, Snake sixth, Horse seventh, Ram eighth, Monkey ninth, Cockerel tenth, Dog eleventh, and Pig twelfth – and last. The Gods said, 'Well done! Each of you will have a year named after you, in the order that you finished the race.' All the animals were happy, because now every New Year would be named after one of them.

Barbara Moore